Financialisation and Development in Asia

Multilateral development agencies have increasingly focused on underdeveloped Asian countries as potential new sites for financial capital. Often referred to as "emerging markets", these economies are seen as ripe for private sector investment and, at the same time, in need of foreign capital to support rapid industrialisation, modernisation and poverty reduction. This confluence of interests suggests a means for quickly closing the "development gap", primarily through mobilising regulatory, institutional and governance reforms designed to reduce barriers to foreign capital, institutional inefficiencies and risks to investment, capital repatriation and market operation. Development agencies thus now encourage the construction of "enabling environments" to support "market driven development" through processes variously identified as "financialisation", centring on the role of the market and private capital. While the state itself has historically occupied a central place in economic development, new financialised modes of development are increasingly marginalising the state, its influence in the economy and thus its ability to manage developmental outcomes. In this volume a collection of leading authors critically assess these developments, highlighting the emergence of financialised modes of development and their contested and often problematic nature. Drawing upon a series of case studies, the contributors explore not just the increasing use of financialised development initiatives, but assess critically their implications in terms of the emergent risks, costs and inequalities that often accompany them.

This book was originally published as a special issue of the *Asian Studies Review*.

Toby Carroll is Associate Professor and Associate Head in the Department of Asian and International Studies at City University of Hong Kong. His research concentrates on the political economy of development, with a particular geographical focus on Asia. He has published in journals such as *Journal of Contemporary Asia*, *Asian Studies Review*, *Globalizations*, *Development and Change*, *Pacific Review* and *Antipode*, and much of his work has been translated into Indonesian. He is the author of *Delusions of Development: the World Bank and the post-Washington Consensus in Southeast Asia* (Palgrave MacMillan) and co-editor (with Darryl Jarvis) of *The Politics of Marketising Asia* (Palgrave MacMillan, 2014). He has edited or co-edited numerous journal special issues (including for *Journal of Contemporary Asia*, *Asian Studies Review* and *Globalizations*). He also co-edits (with Darryl Jarvis, Paul Cammack and M. Ramesh) the Palgrave book series, *Studies in the Political Economy of Public Policy*. He is a co-editor of *Journal of Contemporary Asia* and a thematic editor for *Asian Studies Review* (*Political Economy and International Politics*).

Darryl S.L. Jarvis is Professor and Associate Dean, Faculty of Liberal Studies and Social Sciences at the Hong Kong Institute of Education. His research interests focus on international and political risk, comparative public policy, regulation, infrastructure, and the political economy of investment into Asia. His publications include (co-edited with Toby Carroll) *The Politics of Marketising Asia* (Palgrave Macmillan, 2014); (with Anthony Welch) *ASEAN Industries and the Challenge from China* (Palgrave Macmillan); (with Ed Araral, M. Ramesh and Wu Xun) *Infrastructure Regulation: What Works, Why, and How do we Know? Lessons from Asia and Beyond* (World Scientific); *Handbook of International Business Risk: The Asia Pacific* (Cambridge University Press); *International Relations and the Challenge of Postmodernism: Defending the Discipline* (University of South Carolina Press); (with R.M. Crawford) *International Relations. Still an American Social Science? Toward Diversity in International Thought* (State University of New York Press); and *Post-modernism and its Critics: International Relations and the Third Debate* (Greenwood/Praeger). He has also contributed articles to *Globalizations, Journal of Contemporary Asia, Asian Studies Review, Journal of Asian Public Policy, European Journal of Law and Technology, Regulation & Governance, International Relations, Technology in Society, Energy, Politics and Society, Journal of International Relations and Development, Asian Survey, Global Society: Journal of Interdisciplinary International Relations, Contemporary Politics, The Australian Journal of International Affairs*, as well as authored a series of invited papers.

Financialisation and Development in Asia

Edited by

Toby Carroll and Darryl S.L. Jarvis

Routledge
Taylor & Francis Group
LONDON AND NEW YORK

First published 2015 by Routledge

2 Park Square, Milton Park, Abingdon, Oxfordshire OX14 4RN
711 Third Avenue, New York, NY 10017

Routledge is an imprint of the Taylor & Francis Group, an informa business

First issued in paperback 2018

British Library Cataloguing in Publication Data
A catalogue record for this book is available from the British Library

ISBN 13: 978-1-138-90142-1 (hbk)
ISBN 13: 978-1-138-08293-9 (pbk)

Typeset in Times
by RefineCatch Limited, Bungay, Suffolk

Publisher's Note
The publisher accepts responsibility for any inconsistencies that may have arisen during the conversion of this book from journal articles to book chapters, namely the possible inclusion of journal terminology.

Disclaimer
Every effort has been made to contact copyright holders for their permission to reprint material in this book. The publishers would be grateful to hear from any copyright holder who is not here acknowledged and will undertake to rectify any errors or omissions in future editions of this book.

Contents

Citation Information

The chapters in this book were originally published in *Asian Studies Review*, volume 38, issue 4 (December 2014). When citing this material, please use the original page numbering for each article, as follows:

Chapter 1
Introduction: Financialisation and Development in Asia under Late Capitalism
Toby Carroll and Darryl S.L. Jarvis
Asian Studies Review, volume 38, issue 4 (December 2014) pp. 533–543

Chapter 2
Global Politics of Microfinancing Poverty in Asia: The Case of Bangladesh Unpacked
Heloise Weber
Asian Studies Review, volume 38, issue 4 (December 2014) pp. 544–563

Chapter 3
Innovation and the Entrepreneurial State in Asia: Mechanisms of Bond Market Development
Lena Rethel and Timothy J. Sinclair
Asian Studies Review, volume 38, issue 4 (December 2014) pp. 564–581

Chapter 4
Building a Venture Capital Market in Vietnam: Diffusion of a Neoliberal Market Strategy to a Socialist State
Robyn Klingler-Vidra
Asian Studies Review, volume 38, issue 4 (December 2014) pp. 582–600

Chapter 5
Financialisation through Microfinance: Civil Society and Market-Building in India
Philip Mader
Asian Studies Review, volume 38, issue 4 (December 2014) pp. 601–619

Chapter 6

Market Creation by Leninist Means: The Regulation of Financial Services in the People's Republic of China
Neil Collins and Joern-Carsten Gottwald
Asian Studies Review, volume 38, issue 4 (December 2014) pp. 620–638

Please direct any queries you may have about the citations to
clsuk.permissions@cengage.com

Notes on Contributors

Toby Carroll is an Associate Professor in the Department of Asian and International Studies at the City University of Hong Kong. His research focuses on the political economy of development, with a particular emphasis upon neoliberal agendas in Asia. He is the author of *Delusions of Development: The World Bank and the Post-Washington Consensus in Southeast Asia* (2010), which was nominated for the 2011 British International Studies Association International Political Economy Group prize. His latest book (edited with Darryl Jarvis), *The Politics of Marketising Asia*, has just been published. He is on the editorial boards of *Asian Studies Review* and is a co-editor of *Journal of Contemporary Asia*.

Neil Collins is Dean of the Graduate School of Public Policy, Nazarbayev University, Kazakhstan, and an Emeritus Professor at the National University of Ireland, Cork. He is a past president of the Political Studies Association of Ireland and a former Centennial Scholar at the American Political Science Association in Washington DC. He is the author or co-author of several books, including *Understanding Chinese Politics* (2013).

Joern-Carsten Gottwald has been Professor of East Asian Politics at Ruhr University, Bochum, Germany, since 2011. Prior to his appointment he worked at the Centre for Chinese and East Asian Politics at Free University Berlin, Germany; at the Department of Political Science, University of Trier, Germany; and at the Irish Institute of Chinese Studies, National University of Ireland, Cork, Republic of Ireland.

Darryl S.L. Jarvis is Professor and Associate Dean in the Faculty of Liberal Studies and Social Sciences at the Hong Kong Institute of Education. He has published widely in the areas of international relations, regulatory politics and the political economy of investment issues in Asia. His recent publications include *The Politics of Marketising Asia* (with Toby Carroll); *ASEAN Industries and the Challenge from China* (with Anthony Welch); *Infrastructure Regulation: What Works, Why, and How do we Know? Lessons from Asia and Beyond* (with Ed Araral, M. Ramesh and Wu Xun); *Handbook of International Business Risk: The Asia Pacific*; *International Relations and the Challenge of Postmodernism: Defending the Discipline*; *International Relations: Still an American Social Science? Toward Diversity in International Thought*; and *Post-modernism and its Critics: International Relations and the Third Debate*.

Robyn Klingler-Vidra completed her PhD at the London School of Economics and Political Science, UK, in 2014. She is a Senior Research Fellow at the Coller Institute of Venture at Tel Aviv University, Israel. Her research interests include the development of venture capital markets, financial policy in East Asia, global public policy efforts to localise Silicon Valley, and how policy models transform as they diffuse. Her recent publications include a co-authored article, "Convergence More or Less: Why Do Practices Vary as they Diffuse?" (*International Studies Review*) and an article entitled "The Pragmatic Little Red Dot: Singapore's US Hedge against China" (*LSE IDEAS*). She leads the World Economic Forum's United Kingdom Executive Opinion Survey on global competitiveness, helps teach the LSE undergraduate international political economy course and is an Instructor for LSE Enterprise executive education courses on economic competitiveness and innovation.

Philip Mader is a Post Doctoral Researcher at the University of Basel, Switzerland. His research interests lie at the intersection of the sociology of money and finance with the politics of development and philanthropy. For his doctoral thesis (2012) he was awarded the German Thesis Award and the Otto Hahn Medal. His publications include the edited volumes (with Leonhard Dobusch and Sigrid Quack) *Governance across Borders: Transnational Fields and Transversal Themes* (2013); and (with Gerhard Klas) *Renditemachen und Gutestun? Mikrokredite und die Folgen neoliberaler Entwicklungspolitik*.

Lena Rethel is Associate Professor of International Political Economy in the Department of Politics and International Studies at the University of Warwick, UK. Her current research interests include global financial governance, the relationship between finance and development, and the emergence and rapid expansion of Islamic finance. Empirically, her research is mainly focused on Southeast Asia – in particular financial development in Malaysia, Singapore and Indonesia. Her book *The Problem with Banks* (co-authored with Timothy J. Sinclair) was published in 2012. She is currently working on a new book provisionally entitled *Capital Markets by Design: From Crisis Recovery to Islamic Finance in Southeast Asia*.

Timothy J. Sinclair is Associate Professor of International Political Economy at the University of Warwick, UK, and Professor in the Center for Finance, Politics and History at Kyung Hee University, Seoul, South Korea. He served as an official in the New Zealand Treasury in the late 1980s, giving advice on public expenditure and working on the privatisation of government agencies. His book on the credit rating agencies, *The New Masters of Capital: American Bond Rating Agencies and the Politics of Creditworthiness*, was published in 2005. In 2012 he published *The Problem with Banks*, co-authored with Lena Rethel, and *Global Governance*. His articles have appeared in journals such as *Review of International Political Economy* and *Global Governance*.

Heloise Weber is Senior Lecturer in International Relations and Development Studies in the School of Political Science and International Studies at the University of Queensland, Brisbane, Australia. She has published widely on the global politics of development, inequalities, and poverty reduction strategies, as well as on theoretical and methodological concerns in and around the global political economy of development and inequalities. She is the co-editor (with M.T. Berger) of *Recognition and Redistribution: Beyond International Development* ([2009]/2013) and editor of *Politics of Development* (2014). She is co-author (with M.T. Berger) of *Rethinking the Third World – International Development and World Politics* (2014). She is currently working on a book on the global politics of microcredit and poverty.

Introduction: Financialisation and Development in Asia under Late Capitalism

TOBY CARROLL

City University of Hong Kong

DARRYL S.L. JARVIS

Hong Kong Institute of Education

Abstract: *Multilateral development agencies have increasingly focused attention on underdeveloped countries in Asia as potential new sites for financial capital. Often referred to as "emerging markets", these economies are seen as ripe for private sector investment and, at the same time, in need of foreign capital to support rapid industrialisation, modernisation and poverty reduction. For development agencies, this confluence of interests suggests a means for quickly closing the "development gap", primarily through mobilising techno-managerial modalities designed to reduce barriers to capital entry and other institutional inefficiencies seen as inimical to investment. Thus development agencies now encourage the construction of "enabling environments" to support "market driven development" through processes of "financialisation". Development, in this sense, is no longer state-led or state-centred, but rather financially driven and privately procured.*

As we highlight in this special issue, however, financialised modes of development are highly contested and problematic. Indeed, the diffusion into the underdeveloped world of essentially developed world financialisation agendas that seek to instil a broad-based market rationalism that downloads new costs and risks to populations is of significant concern. This Introduction sets in context and introduces a much needed set of articles that bring clarity to financialisation in developing Asia and its implications for development as a process of substantively improving material conditions.

Introduction

In 2011, several years after the onset of the global financial crisis and amid the ongoing European sovereign debt crisis, the World Bank released that year's Global Development Horizons report entitled *Multipolarity: The New Global Economy.* This report, which appropriated the language of international relations for its title, was an unambiguous statement from the Bank that the global political economy had changed fundamentally and was no longer constituted by the pervasive logic of binary opposites: a developed North and an underdeveloped South. Rather, much of the kernel for ongoing development and economic dynamism was now, in the Bank's view, situated in the global South. The Bank's then Chief Economist, Justin Yifu Lin, noted the characteristics of this unfolding global order:

> The world economy is in the midst of a transformative change. One of the most visible outcomes of this transformation is the rise of a number of dynamic emerging market countries to the helm of the global economy. It is likely that, by 2025, emerging economies – such as Brazil, China, India, Indonesia, and the Russian Federation – will be major contributors to global growth, alongside the advanced economies. As they pursue growth opportunities abroad and encouraged by improved policies at home, corporations based in emerging markets are playing an increasingly prominent role in global business and cross-border investment. The international monetary system is likely to cease being dominated by a single currency. Emerging-market countries, where two-thirds of official foreign exchange reserves are currently held and whose sovereign wealth funds and other pools of capital are increasingly important sources of international investment, will become key players in financial markets. In short, a new world order with a more diffuse distribution of economic power is emerging – thus the shift toward multipolarity (Lin, 2011, p. xi).

Lin's foreword captured a complex though clearly discernible dynamic that had been unfolding for some time but which was now credited with new importance on the back of the global economic crises enveloping much of the world – and, persistently, the developed world.

Names, places and economic spaces

For some time, of course, an increasingly large number of developing countries (including some of the most populous) have been commonly referred to as "emerging markets" (Lin also uses the phrase); a phrase that is in marked contrast to their previous designation as "developing", "underdeveloped" or even "backward" economies. This is not just a change in nomenclature or a relabelling in the face of political correctness. More fundamentally, it signals an ideational shift in the way capital views and values the economic spaces of developing nation-states and the latter's role in late-stage capitalism. No longer are underdeveloped nation-states perceived as spaces of nefarious political projects, corrupt elites or dysfunctional political systems that act as sinkholes for foreign capital and are "no-go" zones because of recurrent political risk. Rather, they increasingly represent nascent markets: home to large populations with predominantly young demographics, where the uptake of goods and services and the need for investment capital represent growth opportunities that advanced, mature economies can no longer sustain due to a combination of market saturation, ageing demographics and the limited growth trajectories of capitalist states. In the space of a single decade, "underdeveloped", "dysfunctional", "backward" states have been "ideationally rehabilitated" into *emerging economies*: places which, as a result of their adoption of neoliberal (market-oriented) norms, provide the institutional and material basis for capital penetration, financialisation, market development and a more orderly set of practices for the management of risk to capital.

The most prominent characterisation of this transition was articulated by the Chief Economist of Goldman Sachs, Jim O'Neill, with his now famous coining of the "BRICs" moniker – to highlight the consolidating economic importance of Brazil, Russia, India and China – in the investment bank's *Global Economics Paper* series. Ten years before Lin's foreword in the World Bank report, O'Neill extrapolated the linear growth projections of BRIC economies and suggested that within a few decades the epicentre of global economic activity would migrate to the global South, catapulting these economies into global economic players of enormous proportions.[1] As O'Neill noted, this raised serious implications for the future structural composition of the global economy, its political architecture, and the locus of global capitalism (O'Neill, 2001, p. s03). Perhaps most importantly for O'Neill and Goldman Sachs were the implications for global business strategy and the sustainability of current global enterprises: whether in financial services, telecommunications, electronics, consumer durables or automobiles, if business was not extensively invested in the BRIC economies in 20 years' time either it would be extinct or its global presence would be marginalised by the size of these fast emerging behemoth economies. In the new mantra of global business strategy, emerging economies were not just marginal markets and adjunct revenue streams; they were the future.

In 2005, O'Neill built upon the uptake of the BRICs euphoria by detailing yet another grouping of countries of interest to investors, the "Next 11". Notably, this time, the grouping included the three most populous Southeast Asian countries: Indonesia, the Philippines and Vietnam. Competing groupings, too, such as the "Civets" (Colombia, Indonesia, Vietnam, Egypt, Turkey, South Africa), detailed in 2008 by the Economist Intelligence Unit's Robert Ward, also trumpeted the importance of countries such as Indonesia (the world's fourth largest country by population) and Vietnam, whose rapid double-digit growth had accelerated the country from abject poverty to the 35th largest economy in the world by 2005 (Moore, 2012; O'Neill, 2001).

What these crude investment categorisations (one of which – the BRICs – also morphed into a political entity) signalled was that those seriously interested in predicting and pitching sources of capital accumulation were looking not just beyond the developed world (the "core"/"North"), but increasingly beyond India and China to other countries that offered the allure of high growth rates, cheap labour, untapped domestic pools of capital, and, importantly, hundreds of millions of new consumers.[2] Under late capitalism the search for growth and profit had prompted a new, at first euphoric and later (with the onset of the global crises) desperate, expansionism – a reality that would simultaneously subsume and subordinate earlier neoliberal agendas to a new, vastly more simplistic mantra of "if it grows it goes".[3]

Neoliberalism, multilateral organisations and shifting power relations

The ideational sea change in attitudes toward emerging economies as an increasingly central facet of global capitalism represents something of a triumph of neoliberalism as a dominant form of global political-economic organisation. Ironically, this sea change also represents one of the greatest challenges to the conventional neoliberal international order, creating a power shift that threatens the viability of extant international institutions and the regime of governance that has been in place since the end of World War II. Previously, for example, the logic of neoliberalism was to penetrate the geographies of untapped states and encourage the adoption of those institutions, norms and rules that comprised a broadly defined "Washington Consensus". In this context, multilateral organisations historically enjoyed what might be termed unilateral leverage over developing countries, where capital shortages allowed lending organisations to impose stringent, and often onerous, conditions, including forms of marketisation, fiscal austerity, the removal of trade/investment barriers and direct/indirect forms of protectionism (see, for example, SAPRIN, 2004). Not surprisingly, these conditionalities were unpopular with borrowing countries as well as a constant source of irritation to multilateral organisations as domestic vested interests and capacity constraints often stalled their implementation.

With the progressive adoption of neoliberal policy norms, specifically the institutionalisation of market relations, capital account liberalisation, currency convertibility, trade liberalisation, and the introduction of state guarantees protecting the rights of investors, neoliberalism's progressive march has transformed this power relationship and the circuits of capital on which it has historically rested. Most recently, for example, the growth of domestic capital markets in the global South, the creation of state investment vehicles (sovereign wealth funds) drawing on models imported from the global North, and the generation of domestic surpluses through increased economic activity, have witnessed many of these economies become net capital exporters. More importantly, this has occurred at the same time as the economic crisis in Europe and the United States has thrown budgets into deficit and increased the demand for long-term borrowing to sustain fiscal expenditures and countercyclical budget measures. As a result, the political leverage and structural power enjoyed historically by multilateral agencies have been eroding, transforming the modality of their operation, their relationships with developing economies, and the policy agendas they pursue.

Acknowledging this reality in early 2012, then-President of the World Bank, Robert Zoellick, offered the following concession in a *Foreign Affairs* piece entitled 'Why We Still Need the World Bank':

> The rise and diffusion of private capital and free enterprise around the world now offered developing countries a great opportunity. Yet that did not obviate the need for the World Bank, because it was never simply about loans and grants: its role has been to contribute to the development of market economies in an open international system – fostering growth, opportunity, and hope and overcoming poverty within a better political and security order...

> To accomplish this mission, the World Bank needed new directions, firmer guidance, and better execution. It had to adapt to *shifts in economic influence, with emerging markets becoming new economic engines and development no longer being about a North-South hegemony.* In developing countries, it needed to assist the private sector – whether investors from abroad or companies at home – to clear away obstacles to entrepreneurship. It needed to foster inclusive and sustainable growth, and shared responsibilities, *within a changed international system.* The job for our leadership teams was to point out the new directions, build support and partnerships, translate the overarching vision into specific actions, remain alert to opportunities to innovate, and execute, execute, execute (Zoellick, 2012; emphasis added).

These "new directions" and "better guidance" – in response to the "if it grows it goes" dynamic – have also been reflected in a broader paradigm shift within development policy itself that Carroll (2012) has described as "deep marketisation". Deep marketisation represents the third wave of a dynamic and historically evolving neoliberal development policy agenda. In the first wave, neoliberal development policy defined a set of prescriptive policy objectives and ideational values about the role of the state in market relations that came to comprise the Washington Consensus. This sought to "roll back" the state, its size, scope and presence in domestic economic activity, not only as a means of reducing the "crowding out" of private sector activity, but in what was seen as a broader means of reducing the impact of corruption or state capture on the polity and economy of developing countries. First-wave neoliberal development policy thus aggressively prescribed privatisation of state-owned assets, capital account liberalisation through floating of currencies, the roll-back of barriers to market entry for domestic and international investors, and a dismantling of import-substitution trade barriers in favour of immersion into export-oriented manufacturing and trade. Rapid "internationalisation" and a dismantling of an omnipresent and rent-seeking state, its adherents argued, would herald impressive growth, economic transformation and modernisation (Williamson, 1990; see also Duménil and Lévy, 2011, p. 16).

Second-wave neoliberal development policy consolidated this ideational program, deploying the institutional apparatus necessary to support market operation through the construction of a regulatory state. Policy prescriptions situated around the post-Washington Consensus (PWC) attempted to "roll out" legal instruments, procedural norms and regulatory capacity as a means of reducing the opacity for opportunistic political intervention that might capture or pose a risk to market operation and capital (Brenner and Theodore, 2002, p. 27; Jarvis, 2012; Jayasuriya, 2000).

The third wave of neoliberal development policy, deep marketisation, by contrast represents a series of policy approaches that are more pragmatic in promoting pro-growth/pro-private sector agendas. Indeed, deep marketisation strategies rely on supplantive orthodoxies that work on, through and around the state in tandem with specific vested interests (classes and capital). Specifically, deep marketisation reflects a new politics of development characterised by the increased leverage of certain political elites and the state in underdeveloped countries with respect to international capital and multilateral institutions. The unilateral leverage multilateral agencies historically enjoyed over developing states – however unevenly – is thus usurped by coextensive class interests that form a powerful constituency comprised of both domestic and international interests. The developing state, however, while largely freed from the binds of multilateral development financing, is increasingly subjected to broad-based market discipline as it is systematically embedded in global capitalist social relations in a more complete manner.

Deep marketisation thus continues the neoliberal project of attempting to constitute capitalism on a truly global scale (Cammack, 2012), while deploying and upgrading "development" modalities that are sensitive to the new politics described above. For example, the ramping up of public-private partnerships (PPPs) of all shapes and sizes presents opportunities for state elites to seemingly offload the headaches of providing services and infrastructure (while gaining legitimacy for "tackling" pressing problems) and at the same time provides profit-yielding opportunities for capital. Consequently, the rigorous promotion of PPPs by the World Bank and others that commenced in the 1990s has taken on renewed vigour as the seemingly only "plausible" policy solution to service and infrastructure provision under late capitalism in the underdeveloped world. Likewise, risk mitigation for capital (including financial capital) – that is the escorting of international capital by multilateral development agencies into frontier and emerging market settings – has itself become a valued form of development policy, making many (often large) infrastructure projects and other investments proceed with alacrity.

Perhaps one of the most consequential developments of deep marketisation, however, has been the large-scale fostering of financial intermediaries and a focus on "access to finance". Access to finance refers to a variety of methods for extending financial capital to the "unbanked" and "underbanked", often via micro, small and medium-size enterprise lending. This last strategy, most prominently championed by the World Bank's private sector arm, the International Finance Corporation (IFC), seeks to expand micro, small and medium-size enterprise sectors by supporting and transforming the financial institutions working with these sectors and bolstering the extension of financial services generally through, for example, the proliferation of mobile and other communication platforms (see Carroll, 2013). To put this work in context, in 2010, the IFC's FI clients provided 8 million microfinance loans and 1.7 million loans to the SME sector. In terms of microfinance financing, these loans were worth just over US$12.5 billion. For SME-related lending the figure was around US$127.8 billion (IFC, 2011, p. 86). To put these figures in context, the total outstanding funds relating to loans and credits of the World Bank's traditional core operations amounted to just over US$233 billion (World Bank, 2012, pp. 20–21).[4]

The modalities of deep marketisation point to a transformation of development policy in line with what is broadly referred to as *financialisation*, a phenomenon that manifests itself through a variety of avenues beyond simply development policy. We use the word financialisation here to refer to the overarching shift from productive to financial forms of capital accumulation (Duménil and Lévy, 2011, pp. 99–112; Foster and Magdoff, 2009; Gunnoe and Gellert, 2010, p. 266), and understand this as a crucial part of what Harvey captured in his description of the transition from a Fordist-Keynesian regime of accumulation dominant in the post-World War II era (centred, however unevenly, upon industrial capitalism, Keynesian economics and nation-states) to a "flexible accumulation" regime now dominant under late capitalism. Flexible accumulation is characterised by increased "flexibility with respect to labour processes, labour markets, products and patterns of consumption" and "the emergence of entirely new sectors of production, *new ways of providing financial services, new markets*, and, above all, greatly intensified rates of commercial, technological, and organizational innovation" (Harvey, 1990, p. 147; emphasis added).

Neoliberalism, of course, has been very closely related to the processes of financialisation, making possible in a regulatory sense many of the spatial and temporal fixes (temporary fixes to crises of accumulation) that have facilitated the ascent of financialisation (Harvey, 2006, p. 415; see also Duménil and Lévy, 2011, p. 18). For example, at both the domestic and international levels, the deregulation of finance and relaxing of capital controls made possible a massive expansion in the influence of financial capital as it sought to yield new sources of surplus outside its traditional domiciles. The pairing of financial liberalisation and increased capital flows to Asia before the 1997 Asian crisis was perhaps the most prominent example of the significant geographic expansion in the reach of finance capital under late capitalism (see, for example, Jomo, 2000, pp. 26–28). Yet the broader switch to flexible accumulation has continued unabated, delivering a near-bewildering array of financialised instruments deployed across a broad spectrum of areas, including environmental management, venture capital promotion, infrastructure and poverty alleviation, and the financialisation of social security through individuated health, disability and retirement contribution systems. All of these have been crucial in the project, following Cammack, to embed competitive capitalist social relations on a truly global scale.

Financialisation and the creation and expansion of new market spaces in Asia

To consider the processes of financialisation and their impact on market creation and expansion and the political economy of Asia's development, it is essential both to capture the breadth of relevant processes (i.e. looking at the variety of ways in which financial forms of capital accumulation are diffusing into "developing" Asia) and to posit an understanding of the relationship between these processes and development – understood in two ways: both as a qualitative shift in material conditions (development's popular meaning) and as a practice associated with activities that fall under the rubric of "development policy". Fortunately, this collection of articles tackles these issues head-on and in a manner that is both empirically rich and theoretically significant.

Indeed, the five contributions in this special issue represent one of the first attempts to collectively assess not just the relationship between financialisation and development, but financialisation's impact on Asia. We think this important for three reasons. First, Asia's development has been coterminous with the evolving waves of neoliberal development policy. It thus represents one of the first regional laboratories into which neoliberal agendas have been diffused and practically realised. Asia, in a sense, is at the cutting edge of this process and the latest phase of deep marketisation, the implications of which are only being realised now. Second, what happens in Asia as a result of the broader dynamics that are also associated with deep marketisation will have global implications, not least because of the increasing centrality of Asia as a crucial economic space in late capitalism. Third, and perhaps most importantly, Asia is home to many of the countries that experienced most dramatically what Richard Higgott (1998, p. 334) described as the "first crisis of globalisation" – the 1997–98 Asian Crisis – a crisis that in many ways was closely associated with neoliberalising reforms, and indeed, financial liberalisation (Jomo, 2000, p. 28). In sum, not only has Asia played host to some of the most important developments and conflicts attending late capitalism and neoliberalism, but what happens in Asia will, we believe, resonate in other developing countries outside of Asia too.

The first contribution by Heloise Weber (2014) delivers a critical assessment of a form of development policy that extends financial discipline to new domains by cultivating new market spaces using microfinance. While microfinance is not new, its recent renaissance has attracted the attention of various development organisations, elevating it to a mainstream "development" modality focused on expanding access to finance. For example, the IFC now has clients on its books responsible for delivering 8 million microfinance loans (a figure predicted to reach more than 24 million in CY2011) worth around US$12.62 billion (IFC, 2011, p. 55, p. 86). Moreover, the sorts of linkages promoted by recent variants of microfinance are vastly more entwined within international capitalist relations than was the case with earlier microfinance programs. By contextualising politically and historically the evolving modalities of microfinance, Weber (2014) details precisely how the creation of new markets – under the rubric of "inclusive finance" – constitutes new disciplinary mechanisms that continue the marketising agenda of earlier structural adjustment programs of the international financial organisations. She points to the implications of this agenda for both non-governmental organisations (NGOs) and development, taking a critical position that urges the reader to understand the politics of the multilateral microfinance agenda and the limits to the constitution of market society.

In the second article, Lena Rethel and Timothy Sinclair (2014) assess the rapid expansion in bond markets in Asia (markets in which public and private entities raise funds to cover their expenditures). Rethel and Sinclair situate the discussion in the context of the "developmental state" which historically has been seen as the vehicle responsible for East Asia's economic success. In the context of late capitalism, however, and third-wave neoliberal agendas such as financialisation and deep marketisation, Rethel and Sinclair assess the challenge financialisation poses to these larger historical projects. In classic analyses of the East Asian developmental state, autonomous bureaucrats often played a pivotal role in allocating resources (including capital), with targeted decisions made to foster fledgling industries. Rethel and Sinclair provide the reader with an interesting case of how the developmental state has been impacted by the unfolding globalisation of capital. They posit that what we are now seeing is the emergence of an "entrepreneurial state", an entity focused on building markets that elsewhere are often left to private institutions. For Rethel and Sinclair, however, this constitutes an important evolution beyond the control of developmental states, with the evolution of Asian bond markets being particularly illustrative of this.

In the third article, Robyn Klingler-Vidra (2014) addresses the theme of institutional diffusion by exploring the substantive transformations that attend the diffusion of global financial markets and their constitution in developing country contexts. Focusing on the constitution of domestic venture capital markets – which many countries have now pursued – Klingler-Vidra charts the experience of the Socialist Republic of Vietnam, attempts at capitalist innovation, and the promotion of small and medium enterprises (SMEs). Vietnam, since embarking upon its *doi moi* ("renovation") reforms in 1986, has been increasingly subsumed within global capitalist relations, especially as a site of production. Klingler-Vidra presents a framework for understanding precisely how the Vietnamese government, advised by international organisations such as the World Bank, has approached the constitution of venture capital markets within an environment in which socialist norms remain influential. The case is particularly intriguing given the lack of direct leverage that international organisations have in a political environment such as Vietnam and where the persistent influence of collectivist and state-centredness exists alongside new capitalist norms.

Philip Mader, in the fourth contribution, returns to the subject of microfinance introduced by Weber. Drawing on a case in India in which microfinance is used in relation to water and sanitation access, Mader (2014) argues that microfinance is not about reducing poverty but, on the contrary, constitutes an attempt to extend and expand capitalist relations of surplus accumulation. He argues that this involves newly "financialised" civil society actors who are central in normalising microfinance as a "development" modality. Moreover, Mader (2014) reminds the reader to consider the unequal social relations of microfinance – especially those between *owners of capital* and *borrowers of capital*. In doing so, he critically assesses the precise manifestations of microfinance and the manner in which it is reshaping social relations in the underdeveloped world on an increasingly significant scale.

The final article in this special issue sees Joern-Carsten Gottwald and Neil Collins (2014) analyse the case of regulating financial services in the People's Republic of China (PRC). The description they provide encapsulates the increasingly common constitution of hybridised market arrangements addressed by many of the contributions to this special issue. Gottwald and Collins demonstrate how the Chinese state attempts to incorporate new protagonists – such as international financial service providers and new regulatory communities – into a regime of financial governance that signals recognition by state elites that while the financialising realities must be accommodated, this accommodation must take place in a manner congenial to the extant configuration of power. In essence, Gottwald and Collins argue that while some may see China's embrace of central bank reform and the establishment of independent regulatory agencies as a step toward the "normalisation" of state-market relations, this is an inaccurate reading. Indeed, on the contrary, for Gottwald and Collins the hybrid state-private sector arrangements emerging in China in relation to financial regulation may well prove to be destabilising to the economic and political order in the long term and make truly globalised forms of regulation complicated, if not impossible to realise.

Taken together, these five papers provide a perspective on the role that financialisation is playing in Asia's development. An important theme that emerges across the contributions is that financialisation is reconfiguring the developmental states of Asia, albeit in uneven and frequently ambiguous ways. Clearly, however, the impact of financialisation is significant, and likely to be far-reaching for decades to come. As editors, we hope that this special issue constitutes something of a springboard to more research on the roles that financialisation, in all its forms, is assuming in re-crafting the public and private spheres and, indeed, the relationship between state and citizen. We also believe that the issue may play a role in a fresh reconceptualising of the nature of the state in Asia under late capitalism. As the tentacles of finance extend into new locales and increase their presence, and as financialised modalities such as microfinance and carbon trading become increasingly normalised as policy tools for development and environmental management, the social and political repercussions of such realities will no doubt only become a more prominent focus for scholars, activists and policymakers alike. We trust that the reader will find in this collection plenty of material, both conceptual and empirical, to advance their scholarly interest and inform their work.

Notes

1. The G7 refers to an industrialised country grouping that includes Canada, France, Germany, Italy, Japan, the United Kingdom and the United States.
2. See, for example, *McKinsey Global Institute* (2012, p. 1); see also *The Wealth Report 2012* (Frank Knight & Citi Private Bank, http://www.thewealthreport.net/The-Wealth-Report-2012.pdf).
3. We would like to credit Tauel Harper for this phrase, which came out of discussions that one of us had with him regarding the global political economy.
4. Total outstanding commitments for the World Bank are calculated by combining outstanding loans and credits for the International Bank for Reconstruction and Development and the International Development Association for the given period.

References

Brenner, Nik and Neil Theodore (2002) Cities and the geographies of "actually existing neoliberalism", in Nik Brenner and Neil Theodore (eds), *Spaces of neoliberalism*, pp. 1–32 (Malden: Blackwell).

Cammack, Paul (2012) Risk, social protection and the world market. *Journal of Contemporary Asia* 42(3), pp. 359–77.

Carroll, Toby (2012) Working on, through and around the state: The deep marketisation of development in the Asia-Pacific. *Journal of Contemporary Asia* 42(3), pp. 378–404.

Carroll, Toby (2013) "Access to finance" and the death of development in the Asia-Pacific. *Journal of Contemporary Asia* (forthcoming).

Collins, Neil and Joern-Carsten Gottwald (2014) Market creation by Leninist means: The regulation of financial services in the People's Republic of China. *Asian Studies Review* 38(4), pp. 620–38.

Duménil, Gérard and Dominique Lévy (2011) *The crisis of neoliberalism* (Cambridge, MA: Harvard University Press).

Foster, John Bellamy and Fred Magdoff (2009) *The great financial crisis: Causes and consequences* (New York: Monthly Review Press).

Gunnoe, Andrew and Paul Gellert (2010) Financialization, shareholder value, and the transformation of Timberland ownership in the USA. *Critical Sociology* 37(2), pp. 1–24.

Harvey, David (1990) *The condition of postmodernity* (Malden: Blackwell).

Harvey, David (2006) *The limits to capital* (London: Verso).

Higgott, Richard (1998) The Asian economic crisis: A study in the politics of resentment. *New Political Economy* 3(3), pp. 333–56.

International Finance Corporation (2011) *IFC Annual Report – I am opportunity* (Washington, DC: International Finance Corporation).

Jarvis, Darryl (2012) Regulatory states in the South: Can they exist and do we want them? The case of the Indonesian power sector. *Journal of Contemporary Asia* 42(3), pp. 464–92.

Jayasuriya, Kanishka (2000) Authoritarian liberalism, governance and the emergence of the regulatory state in post-crisis Asia, in Richard Robison, Mark Beeson, Kanishka Jayasuriya and Hyuk-Rae Kim (eds), *Politics and markets in the wake of the Asian crisis*, pp. 315–30 (London: Routledge).

Jomo, K.S. (2000) Comment: Crisis and the developmental state in East Asia, in Richard Robison, Mark Beeson, Kanishka Jayasuriya and Hyuk-Rae Kim (eds), *Politics and markets in the wake of the Asian crisis*, pp. 25–33 (London: Routledge).

Klingler-Vidra (2014) Building a venture capital market in Vietnam: Diffusion of a neoliberal market strategy to a socialist state. *Asian Studies Review* 38(4), pp. 582–600.

Lin, Justin Yifu (2011) Foreword. *Global development horizons 2011, Multipolarity: The new global economy*, pp. xi–xiii (Washington, DC: World Bank).

McKinsey Global Institute (2012) Available at http://www.mckinsey.com/insights/mgi, accessed 15 January 2014.

Mader, Philip (2014) Financialisation through microfinance: Civil society and market building in India. *Asian Studies Review* 38(4), pp. 601–19.

Moore, Elaine (2012) Civets, Brics and the next 11. *Financial Times* (online edition). Available at http://www.ft.com/intl/cms/s/0/c14730ae-aff3-11e1-ad0b-00144feabdc0.html#axzz2HeJ9oFfZ, accessed 2 October 2012.

O'Neill, Jim (2001) Building better global economic BRICs. Available at http://www.goldmansachs.com/our-thinking/topics/brics/brics-reports-pdfs/build-better-brics.pdf, accessed 5 December 2012.

Rethel, Lena and Timothy J. Sinclair (2014) Innovation and the entrepreneurial state in Asia: Mechanisms of bond market development. *Asian Studies Review* 38(4), pp. 564–81.

Saprin (2004) *Structural adjustment: The SAPRI report* (London and New York: Zed Books).

The Wealth Report 2012 (2012) Frank Knight & Citi Private Bank. Available at http://www.thewealthreport.net/The-Wealth-Report-2012.pdf, accessed 15 Janaury 2014.

Weber, Heloise (2014) Microfinancing poverty in Asia: On the limits of "market society". *Asian Studies Review* 38(4), pp. 544–63.

Williamson, John (1990) What Washington means by policy reform, in John Williamson (ed.), *Latin American adjustment: How much has happened?*, pp. 5–20 (Washington: Institute for International Economics).

World Bank (2012) *Annual report 2012* (Washington, DC: World Bank).

Zoellick, Robert (2012) Why we still need the World Bank. *Foreign Affairs*. Council on Foreign Relations. Available at http://www.foreignaffairs.com/articles/137243/robert-b-zoellick/why-we-still-need-the-world-bank?cid=nlc-this_week_on_foreignaffairs_co-022312-why_we_still_need_the_world_ba_3-022312, accessed 11 January 2012.

Global Politics of Microfinancing Poverty in Asia: The Case of Bangladesh Unpacked

HELOISE WEBER

The University of Queensland

Abstract: *This article offers a critical and systematic political analysis of microfinance schemes linking international, national and local development policy. It substantiates the argument that microfinance schemes are a neoliberal development strategy, primarily advanced to realise a dual purpose: (1) financial sector liberalisation and commercialisation, while extending microfinance as a means to "poverty reduction", and (2) the dampening and undermining of resistance to neoliberal development policies, by relying on the disciplinary potential of these schemes. I illustrate this argument through an examination of the politics of microfinance and development in Bangladesh, which includes analyses of policies prescribed by the World Bank (and also the CGAP). The analysis also draws out the implications (legal and institutional) for many NGOs who have been required to change their status to Microfinance Institutions (MFIs). Microfinance schemes are exemplary of (new) efforts to build markets in Asia in accordance with neoliberal visions of development, and in ways that advance and capitalise on the contradictions of neoliberal development. But they also challenge us to reflect more deeply on the limits of "market society".*

Introduction

My argument about the dual purpose of microfinance is situated within broader debates in political economy about "accumulation by dispossession" (cf. Harvey, 2005), and in this context, the more recent theorising of anti-poverty strategies such as microfinance schemes, as reflective of efforts to mitigate the negative effects of primitive accumulation (Chatterjee, 2008, p. 55). The turn to microfinance is significant politically: it is advanced as a strategy to mitigate the effects of primitive accumulation, but it also incorporates the targeted clients into the circuits of capital as potential micro-entrepreneurs. From the perspective of the advocates of microfinance, the issue is not whether the targeted clients succeed as micro-entrepreneurs. On the contrary, its limits as a poverty-reduction strategy are recognised explicitly by policymakers (see the discussion of Bangladesh below). As I will show, the advance of microfinance (and microcredit) schemes has been premised on the recognition of the potential of such schemes to entrench and manage the contradictions of neoliberal development. Microfinance (and microcredit) schemes have been highly conducive to achieving financial sector liberalisation and commercialisation (Weber, 2002; 2004) but they have also been deployed strategically within the contexts of liberalisation and privatisation programs more generally, with the explicit objective of minimising or containing resistance to the adverse social implications that these policies engender. My analysis explicates how microfinance schemes have been significant to the re-organisation of the global politics of development (Weber, 2002). The example of microfinance is also particularly relevant for illustrating the "making" of private authorities in development. It is premised upon core neoliberal assumptions, both in terms of how poverty is conceived and how it should be resolved.

Microfinance has become a key strategy for poverty reduction globally, at least since the 1980s. As part of the post-Washington Consensus policy framework, it is a preferred approach for international development institutions (including regional development banks), a core component of national development frameworks, and also a key strategy within the operational portfolios of NGOs working in development (which often requires a change in their status to "Financial Intermediaries").

This article offers a critical political analysis of microfinance as a tool for poverty reduction through an approach that integrally locates it within the context of the neoliberal governance of development globally. Microfinance schemes should not be conceived as an extension of neoliberal development, but rather as integral to – constitutive of – the process of neoliberal development itself. I substantiate my critical argument through a detailed examination and analysis of the implementation of a Structural Adjustment Program (SAP) as a development strategy in Bangladesh. The case of Bangladesh is significant for several reasons. First, although not the first "test case" in which microfinance was advanced in the context of a SAP (this was Bolivia, which is also discussed briefly below), the minimalist approach to microcredit as a poverty-reduction strategy arguably evolved in Bangladesh from the inception of the Grameen Bank in the 1980s. Second, as Allister McGregor has argued, since "independence in 1971 the Government of Bangladesh has consistently placed a heavy emphasis upon credit in its rural development strategies" (1989, p. 476). Early critical analyses by McGregor (1989; 1991) of credit in Bangladesh drew links between the advance of micro/credit schemes and the Ohio State University conception of finance in development, the latter being "part of the neoclassical backlash in development economics through the 1970s and 1980s" (McGregor, 1989, p. 467). McGregor argued that the Ohio State conceptions of finance crucially missed the complex social and power relations of development, generally, but especially in Bangladesh. In this context, he argued for an appreciation of the limits of credit interventions as a poverty-reduction strategy and for a better understanding of the broader structures (formal and informal) that sustain and reproduce poverty. Third, there has been no study to date that has presented a systematic and comprehensive account (including in primary sources related to the World Bank in this context) of the role of microfinance in neoliberal development in Bangladesh, despite the emblematic stature of Bangladesh in the microcredit discourse.

One of my foci is the role of the CGAP (the Consultative Group to Assist the Poorest, housed at the World Bank) in setting and coordinating (globally) policy on microfinance in relation to macro-level financial sector liberalisation and commercialisation. It is important to appreciate the role of the CGAP in advancing the commercialisation of finance by linking microfinance to financial markets, but also with regard to the types of rules, regulations and best practices it has developed for the governance of microfinance institutions (MFIs). The discussion of the CGAP has to be selective and I have chosen to focus on key policy directives rather than offering an exhaustive chronological discussion of its institutional development. I show that the CGAP was significant for leveraging regulatory changes in finance in its early stages (especially Phases I and II), and more recently has focused on consolidating these early initiatives and expanding somewhat on these.

The paper offers a detailed account of how the intensified linking of global and local institutional policies in line with neoliberal development has been an integral aspect of the making of "new" markets not least organised by – and for – what Cerny (1997) has called the "competition state". Central to the analysis are the contradictions of this project and the social and political relations it engenders. Thus, in elaborating on the social and political contexts within which microfinance schemes came to be implemented, I identify the significance of social struggles and resistance to neoliberal development and its impact. This is important analytically, as it sheds light on the politics of social change, including policy developments within institutions (cf. Weber, 2006).

By way of a conclusion, I reconnect the critical discussion of microfinance schemes to broader questions about the changing dynamics of the governance of development (global-local linkages) and the deepening of neoliberal discipline organised in the name of "empowering the poor".

Global Finance and Microfinance: Contradictions of Neoliberalisation[1]

According to conventional perspectives, microfinance as an approach to poverty reduction reflects a significant departure from "top-down" policies because it is premised on a strategy that "helps the poor to help themselves". All that was needed, according to the advocates, was the right institutional frameworks at local and national levels that would secure the "enabling environment" to enhance access to finance (credit). This was already the normative basis for the construction of a regulatory regime (globally) of "inclusive finance". The novelty was argued to be the fact that poor people would receive credit without collateral of financial value, but rather based on social collateral (e.g. peer support and peer monitoring). The measure of success of microfinance schemes has been financial performance, with repayment rates the dominant focus. For advocates, microfinance schemes were the most logical extension of neoliberal development, complementing at the community level wider macro-political trends to trade in finance as a key sector (finance is a specific trade sector under the GATS agreement of the WTO).[2] The regulation of microfinance schemes has proceeded in tandem with these macro-political trends with commercial rates of interest at the core (certainly at the level of the targeted "clients"), and with regulatory linkages being developed to link microfinance to global financial circuits and markets. These linkages have been developed not least through the intensified modes of cross-conditionality at the global level (for example, between the WTO and IMF and the WB), and through bilateral and multilateral policies on poverty and development (cf. Weber, 2002; 2004). The potential for microfinance schemes to deliver a "win-win" scenario for all concerned – predominantly the "poor clients", the NGOs working in this sector, and financial institutions – has been stressed as part of the justificatory discourse around them. Indeed, as John Hatch of FINCA stated at the first global microcredit summit in 1997, "it simply doesn't make sense anymore to fight for market shares or steal each other's clients or invade the coverage areas of other microcredit institutions when there are so many potential clients who still have not gained access to microcredit services" (Microcredit Summit, 1997).

From the perspective of a deeper political analysis, however, the "win-win" scenario of microfinance and its association with wider promises of the emancipatory potential of neoliberal development is revealed as an ideological cover for much more complex and highly problematic relations. The global institutional origins of microfinance, as a targeted poverty-reduction strategy, can be traced back to the shift towards neoliberal development in the early 1980s, and specifically to the context of the social and political challenges encountered in efforts to implement Structural Adjustment Programs (SAPs).[3] The social suffering that SAPs created was reflected in rising unemployment because many employed within the formal sector lost their jobs, and since this development occurred together with welfare retrenchment, it generated an increase in the segments of the population that were under- and unemployed but had no access to welfare provisions or "safety nets". The social suffering entailed in efforts to entrench "market society" in ever more comprehensive terms has been manifest in direct social struggles against policies associated with austerity measures. Protests have mainly taken very basic forms such as food riots and more general protests within the target countries, while some have been effective as solidarist protests targeting global governance forums and institutions. Some have accused global governance institutions of "kicking the ladder away" (cf. Chang, 2002) for developing countries, or called for "adjustment with a human face".

From another perspective, however, the protests were perceived as threats that could potentially halt or even reverse the trajectory of SAPs, thus reflecting a political challenge to SAPs specifically, and neoliberal development more generally. Bolivia's 1986 New Economic Program (i.e. a SAP) was the first "test case" of this struggle over neoliberal development, and received significant attention for the potential of social pressure to halt and/or reverse the SAP's process. The Bolivian government, key Bolivian business groups, and the World Bank and the IMF swiftly designed an "Emergency Social Fund" (ESF) to be implemented as part of the SAP's framework. The ESF included microfinance schemes as a key component. It enabled the discourse of SAPs to be shifted from austerity to "being in the name of the poor", thus attempting to gain some legitimacy for the process itself. At the same time, it allowed for the linking of micro- and macro-financial sectors in the logic of commercialisation and liberalisation, an outcome that could not have been more opportunistic from the perspective of those advocating an intensified role for finance in development. The ESF strategy thus came to be replicated in terms of "Social Funds" in the context of the implementation of SAPs in other countries encountering similar challenges.[4] Subsequently, Social Funds were integrated more comprehensively into the World Bank as part of its targeted Poverty Reduction strategy. At the same time, the World Bank redrafted its policy on Financial Sector governance by including microfinance schemes for poverty reduction.[5]

A deeper political analysis of the institutional origins of microfinance schemes thus reveals an alternative account focused on two analytical points. First, resistance to neoliberalisation is identified as a potentially significant political challenge to which disciplinary strategies have been responsive. In this context, microfinance (and microcredit) schemes have been used for their disciplinary potential, which is derived through social pressure (peer pressure) in debt-dependent social relations as well as institutionally designed "methods of rule".[6] These include making it legal for meagre belongings to stand as collateral for credit,[7] and/or requiring NGOs to function within the logic of financial discipline by requiring them to change their formal legal status to that of Financial Intermediaries (FIs). FIs in turn are subject to strict auditing mechanisms. All of these strategies aim to ensure that the governance of development is aligned with the deeper objective of financial sector development in accordance with the commercialisation logic specifically and the relations it engenders, which in turn must be situated within the broader process of neoliberalisation. Second, a focus on social struggles and resistance to neoliberal development offers an intrinsic account of how development is experienced and challenged in the "everyday" (cf. McMichael, 2010, pp. 1–13). This point entails a methodological move, enabling a rendition of the political agency of the "dominated"/subaltern in social and political change, one that necessarily disrupts the progressive narrative of neoliberal development. I return to this point in the concluding section. I now turn to further substantiate this critical argument by examining the politics of the "dual function" of microfinance in the organisation of neoliberal development processes in Bangladesh.

Bangladesh: The "Patron State" of (Micro)Credit[8]

A 1994 World Bank study entitled *Bangladesh: Privatisation and Adjustment* identified privatisation as a "compelling necessity" (World Bank, 1994).[9] In its analysis of the potential for and obstacles to broad-based privatisation and divestiture, the study states that "labour opposition is often regarded within Bangladesh as one of the intractable problems of privatisation" (World Bank, 1994, p. 44). Nevertheless, it concludes that experiences from other countries suggest that this opposition is not insurmountable. The study also recognises that labour is highly politicised in Bangladesh, particularly "in and around Dhaka city" (World Bank, 1994, p. 46). It nevertheless recognises that urban workers often still have rural connections, and anticipates capitalising on these social relations in the context of the adjustment process, while also acknowledging limits to such an approach (World Bank, 1994, p. 45).

The informal sector in Bangladesh already carries almost two-thirds of the workforce, with many struggling to make ends meet. Yet, it is this "sector" that was to absorb the anticipated redundancies. In tackling these policy implications, the study identifies various reactive and proactive measures to overcome the problem of labour opposition to privatisation: one of these is "self-employment oriented credit schemes" (World Bank, 1994, p. 49). The study cites microcredit schemes, and particularly the

Grameen model, as an option to absorb this surplus labour, but explicitly rejects the Grameen model on the basis that it is an inappropriate alternative for the more skilled of the retrenched labour force because of its limited development potential.

> This model may not be equally applicable to industrial workers with diverse pre- and post-migration backgrounds, particularly in the urban context. *Besides, the Grameen Bank type model finances mainly simple-technology low-productivity traditional projects with very limited scale of operation* (World Bank, 1994, p. 51; emphasis added).

The minimal economic impact of microcredit and particularly of the Grameen model has thus been recognised at the highest level. At the same time, however, its strategic potential is drawn upon for the purpose of ensuring that, where possible, labour resistance to the macro-level policy reforms is minimised and/or contained. Thus, the recommendation of widespread use of microcredit as an option to redress the potentially adverse political implications of the SAP is based on the assumption that the redundant workers could quickly be absorbed by the informal sector. Given that more than 80 per cent of those below the poverty line already belong to the informal sector, particularly in the rural areas, the report recommended that the Government of Bangladesh (GOB) consider a "Poverty Alleviation Trust as a mechanism for allowing the informal sector to participate in the privatisation program" as this "could also help win broader support for the Government's privatisation program" (World Bank, 1994, p. 82). The elements of this proposed trust were outlined by the World Bank, and among other recommendations, the following was suggested:

> (a) independence from Government – the trustees must be beyond reproach, be sympathetic to the needs of the informal sector and have sound business skills;

and

> (c) the trustees should be required to coordinate their programs with the GOB; and to link up with other poverty alleviation initiatives including the Palli Karma Shahayak Foundation (PKSF); (World Bank, 1994, pp. 82–83).[10]

In 1996, two years after the World Bank identified microcredit as a potential strategy to appease labour opposition to privatisation, it authorised through the IDA a US$105 million Poverty Alleviation Microfinance Project for Bangladesh (World Bank, 1996b). The motivations of this project as well as its design reflected the appropriation of microfinance as a poverty reduction strategy along the logic of the dual purpose of facilitating financial sector liberalisation and attempting to dampen resistance to neoliberal development. The World Bank's own assessment of, and recommendations for, Social Funds explicitly cite this poverty alleviation microfinance project as exemplary of a Social Funds project (Bigio, 1998, p. 63).

As part of the agreement, the GOB was obliged to contribute an additional US$10 million of its own funds towards the project, thus making up a total of US$115 million (World Bank, 1996b, p. 16). The project, based on microfinance minimalism, was justified in terms of its potential socioeconomic impact by reference to a summary of impact studies of microcredit in Bangladesh.

> These results clearly show that a microfinance program such as the Grameen Bank has not only reached the poor (more than 2 million borrowers) but also helped reduce poverty among the borrowers and generated positive externality in the village economy (World Bank, 1996a, p. 63).

This socioeconomic justification, however, contradicts not only critical findings on Grameen impact (cf. Rahman, 1999), but also the findings of the World Bank's own impact assessments and analysis: it does not acknowledge the "limited scale of operation" of these projects (as noted above). It is also noteworthy that although the People's Republic of Bangladesh was the borrower of the IDA credit, the implementing agency of this Poverty Alleviation Microfinance Project is the Palli Karma Shahayak Foundation (PKSF). According to the terms of the agreement the GOB was to borrow IDA funds and on-lend to the PKSF at 1 per cent per annum for 20 years, with 5 years' grace on repayments (see World Bank 1996b, p. 19, 4.21). The PKSF would in turn on-lend these funds to its Partner Organisations (POs) – eligible MFIs – at interest rates in the range of 3.5 per cent. The POs were obliged then to set a minimum interest rate of 16 per cent, which ensured that they did not lend below the commercial rates (World Bank, 1996b, p. 51); however, they were free to set a final lending rate to beneficiaries (expected to be in the 25–30 per cent range) (World Bank, 1996b, p. i). The PKSF was established in FY90 and has been defined as an "apex financing institution to assist promising small and medium NGOs expand their poverty targeted microcredit programs" (World Bank, 1996b, p. 4). The governing body of the PKSF has included Muhammad Yunus of the Grameen Bank (World Bank, 1996b, p. 4). Although it is "registered under the Companies Act of 1913 as a private non-profit organisation" (World Bank, 1996b, p. 4), according to the World Bank, it

> has been profitable, mostly on account of interest income from term deposits and has pursued a policy to project itself as a sustainable institution for staff morale and to the POs and to avoid decapitalization. The high percentage of assets in investments is, thus, partly a reflection of the profitability objective and partly on account of its conservative lending policies. *While this policy has obviously led to sacrificing the poverty objective*, i.e. higher lending, for the reasons noted earlier it seems appropriate (World Bank, 1996b, p. 6; emphasis added).

For the World Bank, the breach of the poverty alleviation objective is entirely acceptable (if we accept for the moment that the objective of the microfinance program was indeed poverty alleviation). The PKSF has strong selection criteria for its POs (World Bank, 1996b, p. 7): in general it can be concluded that these criteria reflect the core objectives and operational features of the Grameen model. The interest rates charged by the POs to the poor borrowers "are much higher than rates in the formal sector. Effective interest rates range from 25–30 per cent per annum" (World Bank, 1996b, p. 8). This rate, the World Bank tells us, is "15–20 per cent in real terms and 50–100 per cent higher than the highest lending rates of private banks" (World Bank, 1996b, p. 8).

World Bank (IDA) and microfinance for poverty reduction: The context of privatisation and liberalisation

The IDA (World Bank) rationale for the Poverty Alleviation Microfinance Project is stated with reference to the capacity of the project to support the World Bank's twin Country Assistance Objectives (CAS) for Bangladesh – namely, "poverty alleviation and broad based economic growth" (World Bank, 1996b, p. 15). It is important to note that while the Poverty Alleviation Microfinance Project was intended to operate as a cost-effective political safety net and a strategy proactively deployed to counter political resistance to the broad-based privatisation project, it also facilitates the creation of an enabling environment for deregulation at policy level. The rationale for IDA involvement in the project has been underpinned by the broader objective of financial sector liberalisation, in order to facilitate the expansion of the financial services industry (World Bank, 1996b, p. 15).[11]

In order to bring about these financial-sector policy changes, the GOB was also obliged to provide US$5 million of the funds it borrows from the IDA, "on a *grant basis* to the PKSF and the Bangladesh Bank to implement the various components for institution building and broadening the microfinance market" (World Bank, 1996b, p. 16; emphasis added). This Poverty Alleviation Microfinance Project constituted the poverty reduction aspect of the World Bank's overall CAS for Bangladesh. In line with the overall liberalisation objective, IDA support for this project was anticipated (among other issues) to "*bring about a fundamental shift from a grant based system to a loan based system*" with reference to development efforts (World Bank, 1996b, p. 15; emphasis in original). This objective clearly influenced the rationale for the project, as it is stated explicitly that "as a result of this Project, the GOB has decided that all future budgetary funding will be in the form of loans, not grants". Consequently, "two large MFIs (Proshika and BRAC) would be using loans for the first time" (World Bank, 1996b, p. 15). The potential knock-on effect this has on the lending implications to end-borrowers is clear. The Project goes on to provide further justification of this policy transition in terms of an emerging donor consensus:

> IDA staff liaised closely with official bilateral donors and international NGOs who have generously supported these programs. Their views and experience have been reflected in Project design. With grants shrinking and donors emphasising financial sustainability and greater accountability, they see *the Project as a path breaker in shifting microcredit away from a grant based system and in sharpening the emphasis on financial sustainability* (World Bank, 1996b, p. 16; emphasis added).

The primacy of the financial sustainability objective of the Poverty Alleviation Microfinance Project is clearly obvious in that establishing "an efficient mechanism to transfer subsidised funds without penalising the banking system" has been an important aspect of IDA rationale for the Project (World Bank, 1996b, p. 15). The subsidised element of the project funds here refers to the IDA concessional lending to the GOB, the GOB subsidised lending to the PKSF and the PKSF's own subsidised lending to its POs (NGOs and MFIs), but does *not* refer to the interest rate charge set at the level of the poor borrowers, which is extremely high (between 25 and 35 per cent). The implications of this poverty alleviation project are significant, not least because it demonstrates how, in ostensibly responding to the social implications of "adjustment", a strategy is developed to extend the discipline of neoliberal development to those most vulnerable. In this sense, while social suffering is framed primarily in terms of the potential risks it poses for the political project of neoliberalisation these same experiences of vulnerabilities serve as a justification for institutionalising a process for financial "trickle-up" (returns on microcredit investment and/or the benefits of the wider logics it facilitates). Far from poverty being reduced, it is actually increased, reproduced and sustained. The full impact of microcredit (and microfinance) in Bangladesh must be seen in the context of broader social and political relations.[12]

The effects and efforts of microcredit-driven poverty reduction are complex, and include the "disciplining" of NGOs through the requirement that they legally transform into Financial Intermediaries (FIs) that conform to the established commercially oriented rules for microfinance, as for example articulated in the "Pink Book" of the CGAP (see CGAP, 1995b). Wider implications and contexts include re-regulations of welfare regimes, protective labour laws, and banking regulations, which have all been increasingly brought into line with the logic of financial discipline as a core value of "inclusive finance". Importantly, through this approach the under- and unemployed, the "casualties of progress" (McMichael, 2010, p. 1), are written back into the script of development as key "clients" in whose name development (and in this case microfinance) proceeds apace. While social deprivation is organised through neoliberal development, the potential value of those subject to such suffering has not gone unnoticed; instead their very "conditions" are drawn upon as justifications of neoliberal development. Importantly, denied in the formal narrative of microfinance are the deeply heteronomous relations that are constitutive of this process. Instead, these experiences and relations are represented in terms such as "pyramid loans", "consumption smoothing" and/or "cross borrowing".

The next section examines the role of the CGAP as an institution explicitly charged with a mandate to expand and develop regulatory mechanisms for financial sector commercialisation with microfinance at its core.

Deepening Rule through Financial Discipline as a Strategy of Development: The Role of the CGAP

The CGAP was established in 1995 and its *Status Report* of June 1998, under the header 'Why CGAP?' reinforced the merits of microfinance in poverty reduction efforts (CGAP, 1998c, pp. 6–7). It is currently represented as follows: "CGAP is an independent policy and research centre dedicated to advancing financial access for the world's poor. It is supported by over 30 development agencies and private foundations who share a common mission to alleviate poverty" (CGAP, 2012).

CGAP was initially established "for a three year period, with the participation of ten bilateral and multilateral donors" (CGAP, 1998a, p. 1). A review of its operations at the end of its first phase found it to be "…a successful innovation in supporting microfinance development and improving donor activities in micro-finance" (CGAP, 1998a, p. 6). Based on these findings, the CGAP was "renewed by its member donors for an additional five years, starting July 1, 1998" (CGAP, 1998a, p. 3). It has since been renewed again, and is a core "Standard Setting Agency" for the further expansion of financialisation (CGAP, 2011a).

The role of the CGAP is substantial in the drive for financial sector liberalisation and the expansion of new methods (and tools) to enhance access to financial services, especially to the poor. The CGAP proactively seeks partnerships in target countries, specifically with the private sector and not public institutions (state efforts are deliberately bypassed, or utilised as channels to facilitate liberalisation), although it interacts with public sector institutions as a "lobbyist" (and standard setting agency) for liberalisation-centred regulation of finance (and microfinance).

The CGAP Phase I: June 1995–June 1998

Initially, the CGAP did not have a separate identity to the World Bank. It did, however, always have its own internal policies and programs that were overseen by its member donors. The World Bank has been one of the largest contributors to the CGAP's Investment Fund. The CGAP *Policy Paper* originally stated six specific objectives integral to the advancement of the Micro-Finance Program, which continue to constitute its operational framework (CGAP, 1995a). These were restated in slight variation in the CGAP's 1998 *Status Report* (1998c, p. 7) and the following four are particularly interesting for understanding the CGAP's role in financial sector development:

Creating an enabling environment for microfinance: An enabling environment encompasses the promotion of neoliberal and commercially oriented sets of policies for the financial sector linked to microfinance operations. The Bolivian PFP or the Bangladeshi PKSF's criteria that forbid their Partner Organisations (e.g. NGOs) to on-lend to the poorest at interest rates below the national commercial rate could be examples of the latter. "Enabling environment" thus includes assessment of financial sector policy and an overall assessment of potential risk factors that may obstruct or impede microfinance growth and expansion. The legislative environment pertaining to NGO status in general, which would include their capacity to act as financial intermediaries, comprises a further example of factors that may be evaluated in this context.

The dissemination of advice on microfinance best practice: Best practice usually refers to a set of rules and norms that may best contribute to the two criteria for success in evaluating the global microcredit and microfinance agenda: financial viability/institutional sustainability and outreach. Best practice is disseminated to a wide audience, which includes private investors in the capital markets (e.g. CGAP collaboration with the IFC) (CGAP, 1998c, p. 3); grassroots practitioners (NGOs and/or MFIs); global actors (MDBs, donors, other interested parties such as Monsanto); national level (i.e. government) policymakers.[13]

The mainstreaming of microfinance best practice in World Bank and donor operations: Mainstreaming microfinance entails working towards broadening and expanding the World Bank's (and indeed other donors') portfolios of microcredit and microfinance operations along best practice lines. The CGAP may advise the World Bank on appropriate strategies to be pursued to enhance microfinance within its programs and how best to make it acceptable to potential governments. Thus, the CGAP approach would capitalise on the World Bank's capacity to leverage policy changes in the financial sector. In this context, the CGAP also engages substantially in "capacity-building initiatives" at global, regional, national and local levels.

Channelling funds to programs/institutions to help build sustainable specialised institutions: The CGAP provides funds to "broaden and deepen the reach of microfinance institutions that service the poor and strive for sustainability" (CGAP, 1998c, p. 2). The CGAP provides *grants* to support NGOs to start up and scale up their microfinance operations along best practice lines. This support is offered directly at the local level and also indirectly through CGAP-supported national and even regional capacity-building initiatives. The various institutions and agents that receive CGAP grants to "on-lend" are generally referred to as CGAP's Partner Institutions (PIs).[14]

The bulk of CGAP funding according to its policy paper has been directed towards programs in IDA countries,[15] and the majority of this funding was to be in the private sector (CGAP, 1995a).[16] Although the CGAP provides grants and not loans, its portfolio is referred to as the "Investment Fund" (CGAP, 1995a).[17] CGAP will generally provide matching grants to eligible PIs.[18] Interestingly, although the CGAP itself provides grants, it does so on the basis that its PIs will on-lend these grants on a commercial basis, preferably at all levels of the lending structure and with mandatory interest rates for loans made directly to the poor. While CGAP PIs may be diverse, they nevertheless, according to the CGAP, "share a common feature – the potential for massive growth and outreach and steady progress toward commercial viability" (1998c, p. 4). Here, we can recall that the rules for the World Bank (IDA) supported microfinance program (discussed above) are exactly in keeping with the CGAP best practice rules and regulations.

Although the World Bank stands as a quasi-external agency to the CGAP, its key contributions to the CGAP mandate have been less clear-cut, with a significant amount of policy overlap between the two. The CGAP's role as an apex body for creating, adapting and mainstreaming microfinance policy, and acting as a clearing house for "lessons learnt", gives it the status of a "Standard Setting Agency", the key policy provider for other agencies (from IFIs to NGOs) involved with microfinance-led poverty reduction and development efforts.

The CGAP – the World Bank and financial liberalisation

CGAP-World Bank collaboration for financial sector liberalisation has been initiated to date in a selected set of countries. This has been achieved partly through what may be best described as the back-door approach. The CGAP plays a crucial role in designing capacity-building initiatives for microfinance, in the words of the CGAP, by "taking advantage of its special status as a neutral multi-donor body with a *technical focus*" (CGAP, 1998c, p. 3; emphasis added). This strategic approach has enabled it to take advantage of the capacity of the World Bank to leverage financial sector policy changes from governments. The "CGAP Secretariat is able to draw policymakers'" (of the World Bank) attention to microfinance, which in turn can be used as a reason to argue for financial sector liberalisation. Since the late 1990s the CGAP has guided such efforts from Tanzania to "Brazil, China, Ethiopia, Peru, Vietnam, and nine West African countries" (CGAP, 1998c, p. 2). In a similar approach, the World Bank (and by extension the CGAP) helped to bring about policy shift towards financial sector liberalisation in nine West African countries: "MFIs subject to the Law on Usury were urged by UEMOA Ministries of Finance to seek an exemption from the ceiling by approaching their respective Ministry" (CGAP, 1997a, p. 7). This outcome transpired despite "little consensus, [however] between practitioners and authorities from the UEMOA countries on the new Credit Union Law".[19]

Indeed, the decision to locate the CGAP Secretariat within the World Bank was based on the recognition of the fact that "through its policy dialogue with governments, the [World] Bank is in an excellent position to influence macroeconomic and financial sector policy" (CGAP, 1998c, p. 22). To this end, the CGAP has "collaborated on World Bank projects in several countries to *leverage the Bank's ability to create enabling policy environments*" (CGAP, 1998c, p. 24; emphasis added).

The World Bank has made good progress with the CGAP in facilitating an enabling environment for microfinance: the outcome has been expedited financial sector liberalisation (CGAP, 1998c p. 24), achieved through "policy dialogue" with governments of the South. The World Bank has complemented its strategy of policy dialogue in leveraging the re-regulation of national policies through the recasting of its Operational Directive (OD 8.30) on Financial Sector Operations. OD 8.30, established in the early 1990s, had set the precedent for the Bank to fundamentally recast financial sector operations in the direction of the liberalisation trend. "Due to uncertainty about how to implement the guidelines into practice" (CGAP, 1997b), however, OD 8.30 was recast as an Operational Policy (OP 8.30) in 1998. The new OP 8.30 has been drafted specifically to directly tie microfinance to global financial sector objectives. This outcome is consistent with the World Bank's commitment to work towards this objective through leveraging other sets of policy tools, in addition to the policy dialogues. Thus, in similar fashion to the CGAP, the World Bank also pursues a combination of non-lending and lending tools to achieve financial sector liberalisation.

The World Bank's redrafting of OD 8.30 reflects these commitments. The main objective of OP 8.30 on FIL (Financial Intermediary Lending) is to establish private or semi-national financial intermediaries (FIs) in relevant countries (World Bank, 1998). The role of the FIs would be to on-lend or extend the process of FIL in-country, based upon the World Bank's FIL criteria.[20] (MFIs may be considered to be FIs.) In the recasting of its policy on financial sector operations, the World Bank effectively set out the direct lending strategy for the implementation and operation of microcredit and microfinance projects/programs. From a top-down perspective, OP 8.30 has managed to incorporate microcredit effectively into broader financial sector objectives by anchoring the FIL approach in the context of poverty reduction. From a bottom-up perspective, it has justified the creation of the enabling environment for microcredit – namely, broader financial sector liberalisation.

CGAP Phase II: July 1998–FY 2002

CGAP's mission has remained the same under Phase II (CGAP2): "to significantly expand very poor people's access to quality financial services from sustainable or potentially sustainable microfinance institutions". Its new strategy, however, was "anchored on building MFI retail capacity in order to achieve its mission" (CGAP, 1997c). This was based on a "key assumption … that the lack of retail institutional capacity is the single largest constraint to rapid expansion of micro-finance services" (CGAP, 1999). The CGAP mandate contained five strategic themes for pursuit of its mission under Phase II. Three of these themes may be identified as extensions of Phase I operations and two may be considered additions (CGAP, 1997c).

Phase I extensions into Phase II
Institutional development
Support changes in member donor practices
Improve the legal and regulatory framework for microfinance

New strategic themes of Phase II
Increase understanding on depth of poverty outreach of microfinance services
Facilitate the "commercialisation" of the microfinance industry

The CGAP during the first year of Phase II (1998–99) worked on these five themes, building on its efforts under Phase I. While some of the approaches were merely extended, other policies were given additional edge. For example, on the issue of institutional development, the CGAP funds were now made available primarily to private institutions (at all levels of the lending structure). In addition to prospective PIs being in the private sector, the majority of their clientele needed to be poor and include as a minimum 50 per cent women. The PIs also needed to have proven that they had successfully achieved significant scale (at least 3,000 clients) in their existing portfolios. In addition, they had to show potential to achieve outreach and financial viability (CGAP, 1998d).

Yet the CGAP concedes that as of June 1998, it "*did not have a practical yardstick for the measurement of poverty*".[21] Thus, the new addition on understanding poverty should be read in the context of this limitation. Here, the CGAP makes reference to what must be one of the most fundamental questions of microfinance and poverty reduction – the issue of impact. At the end of its fourth year of promoting microfinance for poverty reduction, the CGAP stated that questions such as "how poor are microfinance clients?" and "what is the impact of microfinance on poor clients?" remained unanswered (CGAP, 1999, p. 4).

In the first year of CGAP2, 85 per cent of its funds were allocated to institutional development and approximately 3.5 per cent toward commercialisation. By comparison, the low level of direct spending to facilitate commercialisation of the microfinance industry was based on the fact that a "better understanding of the players and issues surrounding this theme" was needed before CGAP fully launched this initiative. Also note that "donors such as USAID and the Inter-American Development Bank [were] already spearheading a fair amount of work in this area" (CGAP, 1999, p. 23). Although the direct lending instruments have been relatively small for commercialisation, CGAP2 has made membership of the Consultative Group conditional upon donors committing to the CGAP mission and policy approach. Thus, for example, the CGAP guidelines for 'Selecting and Supporting Intermediaries' ('Pink Book'; see Chapter 1) must now be adopted officially. This 'Pink Book', based upon microfinance minimalism, effectively set out a clear commercial approach for policy on microfinance. Thus, commercialisation has been achieved through *converging* donor policy across the board with microfinance "best practice".

CGAP2 furthered some of the key strategies adopted in its second phase. At the global level CGAP2 involved "itself in a few selective activities based on 'targets of opportunity'" (CGAP, 1999, p. 21). In this sense, donor-coordination under Phase I was intensified to the extent that the CGAP may "consider whether it can selectively take on a leading role at the country level" on the basis that such a positioning of the

CGAP can have "benefits in terms of harmonising done or programming and promoting *agreement on standards and policies with governments"* (CGAP, 1998b, p. 9; emphasis added). To this effect, potential country choices may be taken proactively by the Secretariat and were based on the perceived strategic importance of particular countries to the donors/MDBs. These decisions will also be based on the potential of the CGAP involvement to create a "demonstrative" (e.g. catalytic) impact, which the CGAP relies on to legitimate microfinance expansion.

In sum, the core regulatory mechanisms of the CGAP were developed in the first two phases. These included influencing the re-writing of the World Bank's financial sector policy. By early 2005 microfinance was already mainstreamed within most "developing" countries. At the same time, the guidelines and best practice were also mainstreamed, with significant implications for NGOs whose status needed to be changed to MFIs and FIs globally.

The CGAP in 2011: New directions in the deepening of financial instruments

A recent 'White Paper on Global Standard-Setting Bodies and Financial Inclusion for the Poor' makes a couple of extremely important new recommendations. For instance, this White Paper links access to finance, and lack thereof, to questions of security and violence, arguing however that the benefits of "inclusive finance" outweigh its negative effects (which include conflict as a result of the effects of pyramid loans). More important, though, is how the White Paper sets the standard for what an effective financial institution ought to be. According to this document (8):

> "Financial Inclusion": A Working Definition
>
> "Financial inclusion", as the term is used in this white paper, refers to a state in which all working age adults, including those currently excluded by the financial system, have effective access to the following financial services provided by formal institutions: credit, savings (defined broadly to include current accounts), payments, and insurance.
>
> "Effective access" involves convenient and responsible service delivery, at a cost affordable to the customer and sustainable for the provider, with the result that financially excluded customers use formal financial services rather than existing informal options.
>
> "Financially excluded" refers to those who do not have access to or are underserved by formal financial services…
>
> "Formal institution" refers to a financial service provider that has a recognised legal status and includes entities (and, in some countries, even some individuals) with widely varying regulatory attributes, subject to differing levels and types of external oversight. However, the fact that a customer's financial service provider has a recognised legal status does not mean she or he should be considered "financially included" under the definition used in this white paper: for this, all the conditions of "effective access" must be met.

Effectiveness here must be understood in terms of the commercialisation logic of the governance of finance, reaching beyond the regulation of finance and into broader "methods of rule"[22] that attempt to command social relations in more comprehensive ways. It is thus interesting to observe how the question of "formalisation" is conceptualised in the White Paper (CGAP, 2011a, p. 29):

> This makes the question of formalisation a complicated one: in many situations, closing off access to informal financial services because the providers cannot or do not want to meet the requirements of formalisation runs counter to the overall objective of financial inclusion to improve the well-being of poor households. Indeed, there is a strong justification for permitting certain small institutions (such as small financial cooperatives that pose no systemic threat) to operate informally if their members have no access to safer options (Christen, Lauer, Lyman and Rosenberg, 2011; cited in CGAP, 2011a, p. 29).

The "permitting" of small financial cooperatives to operate informally as long as they pose "no systemic threat" insofar as they are not part of "terrorists' money laundering" schemes may well be what is intended here.[23] Equally, one could ask whether "large financial cooperatives" would or should also be considered a systemic risk? My point here is whether what is really at stake is the potential political threat that cooperatives pose for "financial inclusion" as conceived in terms of commercialisation.

Concluding Thoughts: Methodological Considerations

The analysis I have put forward about the dual purposes of microfinance, as a specific example of contemporary development, can really only be wholly comprehended within a wider context of the historically specific neoliberal variant of capitalist development. Through my critical analysis I have shown how neoliberal development has been organised through efforts to accumulate capital and create the conditions for capital accumulation in ways that were not previously anticipated. At the same time, those subject to deprivation through development cannot be merely conceived in apolitical terms (as subjects without the capacity to struggle against such deprivations) but rather as subjects with agency – political agency. That their agency was un- or under-recognised as such in both Liberal and Marxist accounts of social change indicates the need for more creative perspectives on social struggles and social and political change (for a critical appraisal see McMichael, 2008; 2010). As noted in the beginning of this article, Partha Chatterjee (2008) argued recently along these revisionist lines that we were not merely (re)encountering primitive accumulation, but a revised approach that took into account attempts to mitigate the effects of primitive accumulation through anti-poverty strategies. While this is not a wholly inaccurate perspective on anti-poverty strategies generally, the politics underlying microfinance schemes is still somewhat different.[24] According to my analysis, microfinance does more than attempt to reverse the political effects of primitive accumulation. On the one hand, as McMichael (2010, p. 1) has argued, the "casualties of progress" are framed as external to the development project and through this re-framing the alleviation of the conditions of poverty is presented as quite central to the justification of the narrative of progress more generally (McMichael,

2010, p. 1). On the other hand, the microfinance approach constitutes both a form of primitive accumulation and a justification of additional rules and practices that facilitate primitive accumulation through the deepening of the financial agenda specifically and neoliberal development more generally: thus, it is more than a strategic component of neoliberal development – rather, one could argue that it is constitutive. In this sense, the "reserve army" actively created through neoliberal development and modernisation drives appears to serve the functions of both "exchange value" and "use value".[25]

This article's argument about the dual purposes of microfinance is global in scope, although I have shown in detail how this was organised in the context of Bangladesh, aligned with and designed to locally-specific social and political relations. The general trend, regionally and globally, has been, I argue, similar to that of the political analysis of Bangladesh developed in this paper. The role of the World Bank in advancing policy on microfinance, and the role of the CGAP, are not limited to specific country cases, but are of global reach and scope. In turn, these policies align with the broader trend toward neoliberal development in the ideological frame of the "competition state" (Cerny, 1997). My analysis exemplifies efforts to implement "market society" (cf. Polanyi, 2001[1957]) and it should also raise questions about the limits of market society – ethically, socially, ecologically, politically. The social movement protests of recent times should be a useful analytic and normative frame of reference; among other things, social struggles disclose the source of political contestation of development (Weber, 2009). The epistemic underpinnings of these struggles can help us identify the injustices of "market society" and its limits, and thus also provide a better understanding of social and political conflict as located within, rather than being external to, relations of development.

At the same time, the "transnational" relations of development and its contradictions challenge us to re-think how we conceive of development as social change. I have not addressed this question in any detail in this paper, but merely present it here as an important methodological point.[26] How relations (including through institutions) have been linked globally through finance and credit, as well as the challenges this engenders in development more generally, cannot be adequately grasped or explained from the vantage point of established methods of analysis. This raises the point of the inadequacy of using the routinely presumed pre-eminent unit of analysis (i.e. the territorial state) to understand the social and political relations of development (cf. Saurin, 1995). The other methodological challenge concerns the continuing practice of framing poverty as an "original condition"[27] rather than a social relation. In the cases of these two persistent methodological shortfalls the actual relations of heteronomies are concealed rather than revealed.

Acknowledgments

I am thankful to two anonymous referees for useful comments and feedback on a previous draft of this paper. I would especially like to thank one of the referees for thoughtful suggestions generally, and also for the point about the need to strengthen the set-up of this paper by making more explicit the reasons for the focus on Bangladesh. I am also thankful to Martin Weber for comments on various drafts. Sharinee Lalit Jagtiani provided really helpful editorial support for which I am very grateful. A previous draft of this paper was originally presented at a workshop on 'Rethinking Markets in Asia' at the National University of Singapore in 2011. I express my thanks to participants in this workshop. I wish to sincerely thank Darryl Jarvis and Toby Carroll for organising the workshop and for inviting me to participate. Last but not least, I wish to thank the editors of *ASR*, and particularly Michael Barr for his close reading of the final draft of the piece.

Notes

1. This resonates with the early critical analysis of neoliberal politics advanced by Peck and Tickell (2002), which made the case for a "process based analysis of neoliberalisation", as well as their analysis of "roll-out" neoliberalism. See especially pp. 383–92.
2. These have been examined in detail elsewhere (cf. Weber, 2004; 2002).
3. This political agenda coincided with the World Bank's shift to target women for development, including with microfinance schemes (cf. Rankin, 2001).
4. For accounts of the politics of microfinance in such contexts see Elyachar (2002), Rankin (2001), Lazar (2004), Meideros (2001), Goldstein (2005) and Didem (2009). Bateman (2010) also offers an interesting critical analysis of microfinance as a neoliberal strategy. Taylor (2012) links microfinance schemes to the crisis of poor farmers in Andhra Pradesh.
5. For a detailed examination of this see Weber (2004).
6. I am drawing on McMichael (2012), who has argued that "Development is not just a goal; it is a method of rule" (p. 50).
7. For example, "under a 1993 banking law, Bolivia has begun licensing a new class of [financial] intermediaries: Private Financial Funds (PFFs). PFFs were designed to provide financial services to micro- and small enterprises, as well as loans to individuals for purchases of durable goods... Unlike conventional banks, PFFs are permitted to accept non-traditional collateral such as jewellery or furniture" (CGAP, 1994, p. 3).
8. I am borrowing from McGregor's (1989) excellent early critique of credit and finance in development. He uses the term "patron-state" to understand credit relations in Bangladesh not in a "judgemental sense" (p. 479) but because of the significance of "patron-client" relations through which credit filters (p. 481).
9. This report (p. 8) refers to an April 1993 Aid Group Meeting and states that "the understanding for FY94 is that the GOB would accelerate privatisation of SOEs". This report also states categorically that "the GOB needs to issue a Privatisation Policy statement which clarifies its privatisation objectives and expresses its clear commitment to the program... The announcement must be accompanied by a public education program on the benefits of privatisation" (p. 25). It also states that "a public relations program is required to build a broad-based support for the program" (p. 26).
10. For the sake of brevity, I omit points b), d) and e) here.
11. For this overall policy objective, see also World Bank (1996a, esp. pp. 43–47).
12. McGregor (1991) provides a good critique of the "narrow" notions of credit impact, and reinforces the need to get away from what he terms "mickey-mouse" studies of "impact". See esp. p. 3, p. 23 and p. 43.
13. For a detailed list of CGAP's external "consultants", which include Citicorp Foundation and the Bankers Trust Company, see CGAP (1998c, p. 17).
14. For more on the way in which the CGAP has categorised its PIs, see CGAP (1995a).
15. CGAP, 1995a: See Annex 1, paragraph 1, on Eligibility Criteria of the Participating Institutions (PIs).
16. CGAP, 1995a: Annex 1, paragraph 2, on Eligibility Criteria of the Participating Institutions (PIs).
17. CGAP, 1995a: Annex 1 on Eligibility Criteria of the Participating Institutions (PIs), although paragraph 8 of this document does not exclude the possibility of the CGAP providing loans.
18. CGAP, 1995a: See Annex 1 on Eligibility Criteria of the Participating Institutions (PIs). See paragraph 27 on Use of Funds.
19. CGAP, *Newsletter*, No. 3, p. 8. The "UEMOA is the Economic and Monetary Union of the following seven West African nations: Benin, Burkina Fasa, Cote d'Ivoire, Mali, Niger, Senegal, and Togo" (1999, p. 22).

20. In terms of the stated eligibility criteria for potential FIs, the Bank requires assurance that FIs acting as on-lenders in FIL and other investment operations are viable institutions, with, among other criteria "adequate managerial autonomy and commercially oriented governance" (see paragraph 9), which is particularly relevant when state-owned or state-controlled FIs are involved.
21. CGAP (1998d). See note 1 on poverty measurement and note 2 on "operational self-sufficiency".
22. I am drawing on McMichael's argument that "Development is not just a goal; it is a method of rule" (2012, p. 50).
23. This White Paper is part of the G20 initiative of the Financial Inclusion Action Plan (approved in 2010).
24. Chatterjee actually draws on the example of microfinance to argue that such anti-poverty programs "may be regarded as direct interventions to reverse the effects of primitive accumulation". He also states that they are "not driven by the motive of further accumulation of capital but rather by that of providing the livelihood needs of the debtors – that is to say, by the motive of the reversal of the effects of primitive accumulation" (2008, p. 55). To the extent that part of the motivations for microcredit schemes is the substitution of credit for welfare (or decent work), this point could stand. But when situated in the context of in-depth political analysis it is much more problematic.
25. For an interesting account of how the vulnerabilities of "microfinance clients" are perceived from the perspectives of the advocates of microfinance, see CGAP (2011b, p. 4).
26. I have been working on articulating this point about method in the analysis of development, drawing especially on the work of Philip McMichael and Julian Saurin; see Weber (2007).
27. See, for example, McMichael (2005a; 2005b; 2008); see also Nandy (2002).

References

Bateman, Milford (2010) *Why doesn't microfinance work? The destructive rise of local neoliberalism* (London: Zed books).

Bigio, Anthony G. (1998) *Social funds and reaching the poor – Experiences and future directions* (Washington, DC: World Bank).

Cerny, P.G. (1997) Paradoxes of the competition state: The dynamics of political globalization. *Government and Opposition* 32(2), pp. 251–74.

Chang, Ha Joon (2002) *Kicking away the ladder – Development strategy in historical perspective* (London: Anthem Press).

Chatterjee, Partha (2008) Democracy and economic transformation in India. *Economic and Political Weekly* XLIII(16), pp. 54–62.

CGAP (1994) *Focus No. 4* (Washington, DC: CGAP Secretariat, World Bank).

CGAP (1995a) A policy framework for the Consultative Group to Assist the Poorest (CGAP) – A microfinance program. Policy document, 5 September.

CGAP (1995b) *"Pink Book" – Micro and small enterprise finance: Guiding principles for selecting and supporting intermediaries*. Produced by Committee of Donor Agencies for Small Enterprise Development and Donors' Working Group on Financial Sector Development (Washington, DC: World Bank).

CGAP (1997a) *Newsletter*, No. 3, 31 January (Washington, DC: World Bank). Available at http://www-wds.worldbank.org/external/default/WDSContentServer/WDSP/IB/2000/02/24/000094946_99031910545987/Rendered/PDF/multi_page.pdf, accessed 11 October 2012.

CGAP (1997b) A review of the World Bank's microfinance portfolio. Pamphlet (Washington, DC: World Bank).

CGAP (1997c) "CGAP Phase II", starting July 1, 1998 for a period of five years (Washington DC: CGAP Secretariat, World Bank).

CGAP (1998a) *Focus No. 1*, revised September (Washington, DC: CGAP Secretariat, World Bank). Available at http://pdf.usaid.gov/pdf_docs/PNACL638.pdf, accessed 11 October 2012.

CGAP (1998b) Recommendations for the future. Review/Renewal and Governance Committees, 16 January (Washington, DC: CGAP Secretariat, World Bank).

CGAP (1998c) *Status report – Consultative Group to Assist the Poorest* (Washington, DC: CGAP Secretariat, Word Bank).

CGAP (1998d) *"CGAP Phase II": Announcement of funding policy* (Washington: DC: CGAP Secretariat, Word Bank).

CGAP (1999) Annual Report, July 1998–June 1999. Available at http://www.cgap.org/publications/cgap-annual-report-1999, accessed via new link 20 October 2012.

CGAP (2011a) Global standard-setting bodies and financial inclusion for the poor: Towards proportionate standards and guidance. White Paper. Available at http://www.cgap.org/publications/global-standard-setting-bodies-and-financial-inclusion-poor, accessed 20 October 2012.

CGAP (2011b) Too much microcredit? A survey of the evidence of over-indebtedness. *Occasional Paper 19* (Washington, DC: CGAP, World Bank).

CGAP (2012) About CGAP. Available at http://www.cgap.org/about, accessed 14 October 2012.

Didem, Gurses (2009) Microfinance and poverty reduction in Turkey. *Perspectives on Global Development and Technology* 8(1), pp. 90–110.

Elyachar, Julia (2002) Empowerment money: The World Bank, non-governmental organisations and the value of culture in Egypt. *Public Culture* 14(3), pp. 493–513.

Goldstein, Daniel M. (2005) Flexible justice – Neoliberal violence and "self-help" security in Bolivia. *Critique of Anthropology* 25(4), pp. 389–411.

Harvey, David (2005) *A brief history of neoliberalism* (New York and Oxford: Oxford University Press).

Lazar, Sian (2004) Education for credit – Development as citizenship project in Bolivia. *Critique of Anthropology* 24(3), pp. 301–19.

McGregor, Allister (1989) Towards a better understanding of credit in rural development: The case of Bangladesh, the patron state. *Journal of International Development* 1(4), pp. 467–86.

McGregor, Allister (1991) A study of credit, development and change in rural Bangladesh. PhD thesis, University of Bath.

McMichael, Philip (2005a) Globalization, in Thomas Janoski, Robert Alford, Alexander Hicks and Mildred A. Schwartz (eds), *The handbook of political sociology: States, civil societies and globalization*, pp. 587–606 (New York: Cambridge University Press).

McMichael, Philip (2005b) Book Review: The end of poverty: Economic possibilities for our time. *Journal of Comparative Sociology* 46(4), pp. 347–55.

McMichael, Philip (2008) Peasants make their own history… But not just as they please… *Journal of Agrarian Change* 8(2–3), pp. 205–28.

McMichael, Philip (2010) *Contesting development – Critical struggles for social change* (New York and Oxon: Routledge).

McMichael, Philip (2012) *Development and social change: A global perspective*, 5th edition (Los Angeles and London: Sage Publications).

Meideros, Carmen (2001) Civilising the popular? The law of popular participation and the design of a new civil society in 1990s Bolivia. *Critique of Anthropology* 21(4), pp. 401–25.

Microcredit Summit (1997) Closing Plenary. Audio Recording (tape no #070). Audio Recording Services Inc., Maryland.

Nandy, Ashis (2002) The beautiful, expanding future of poverty: Popular economics as a psychological defense. *International Studies Review* 4(2), pp. 107–22.

Peck, Jamie and Adam Tickell (2002) Neoliberalizing space. *Antipode* 34(3), pp. 380–404.

Polanyi, Karl, ed. (2001[1957]) *The great transformation – The political and economic origins of our time* (Boston, MA: Beacon Press).

Rahman, Aminur (1999) Micro-credit initiatives for equitable and sustainable development: Who pays? *World Development* 27(1), pp. 67–82.

Rankin, Katharine (2001) Governing development: Neoliberalism, microcredit and rational economic woman. *Economy and Society* 30(1), pp. 18–37.

Saurin, Julian (1995) The end of international relations? The state and international theory in the age of globalization, in John MacMillan and Andrew Linklater (eds), *Boundaries in question – New directions in international relations* (London: Pinter).

Taylor, Marcus (2012) The microfinance crisis in Andhra Pradesh, India: A window on rural distress. *Food First Backgrounder* 18(3). Available at http://www.foodfirst.org/en/publications/backgrounders, accessed 20 October 2012.

Weber, Heloise (2002) The imposition of a global development architecture: The example of microcredit. *Review of International Studies* 28(3), pp. 537–55.

Weber, Heloise (2004) The new economy and social risk: Banking on the poor? *Review of International Political Economy* 11(4), pp. 356–86.

Weber, Heloise (2006) A political analysis of the PRSP initiative: Social struggles and the organization of persistent relations of inequality. *Globalizations* 3(2), pp. 187–206.

Weber, Heloise (2007) A political analysis of the formal comparative method: Historicizing the globalization and development debate. *Globalizations* 4(4), pp. 559–72.

Weber, Martin (2009) Understanding and analysing social movements and alternative globalization, in Patrick Hayden (ed.), *Ethics and international relations*, pp. 427–42 (Surrey: Ashgate Publishing Limited).

World Bank (1994) *Bangladesh – Privatisation and adjustment* (Washington, DC: World Bank).

World Bank (1996a) *Bangladesh – Rural finance* (Washington, DC: World Bank).

World Bank (1996b) *Bangladesh – Poverty Alleviation Microfinance Project* (Washington, DC: World Bank).

World Bank (1998) Operational Policy 8.30 (OP 8.30): Financial Intermediary Lending (FIL). *World Bank Operational Manual.* Available at http://web.worldbank.org/WBSITE/EXTERNAL/PROJECTS/EXTPOLICIES/EXTOPMANUAL/0,,contentMDK:20064580~menuPK:64701637~pagePK:64709096~piPK:64709108~theSitePK:502184,00.html, accessed 11 October 2012.

Innovation and the Entrepreneurial State in Asia: Mechanisms of Bond Market Development

LENA RETHEL

University of Warwick

TIMOTHY J. SINCLAIR

University of Warwick/Kyung Hee University

Abstract: *Bond markets have expanded rapidly in emerging East Asian economies in recent years. Asian policymakers have played a pivotal role in this development. This process presents an interesting challenge to the developmental state literature associated with bank-based financial systems. We argue that it is best to understand the role of the state as an entrepreneurial state in the construction of these markets, focusing on institutional innovation in three mechanisms of state-led market infrastructure: national or local credit rating agencies, mortgage corporations and bond pricing agencies. National credit rating agencies rate the creditworthiness of debt in local currency. Mortgage corporations create markets in securitised housing loans. Bond pricing agencies put a value on illiquid debt instruments to enable mark-to-market portfolio management. Together, these three mechanisms constitute the core determinants of the market (demand for creditworthy products, supply of tradeable assets, and the fixing of a price to those assets). In so doing they influence the nature of market operations, producing outcomes very different from the free market ideal type. We also consider cross-country commonalities and variations in this general pattern.*

Introduction

Emerging East Asian bond markets have expanded rapidly in recent years, and governments have played a pivotal role in this development. Bond market development has been encouraged by governments as a way to mitigate the risks associated with increased international capital mobility and as a means of channelling savings towards economic growth. This process presents an interesting challenge to the developmental state literature associated with bank-based financial systems, which sees bond markets at best as being of marginal significance (see, for example, Öniş, 1991; Wade, 2004; Amsden, 1989). Indeed, we suggest that bond market development should be seen as an integral part of the ongoing process of state transformation in the region (see also Hameiri, 2012).

By focusing on institutional innovation, this article introduces the concept of the "entrepreneurial state" as an aid to understanding the role of government in the construction of these markets. Economic analysis typically suggests that markets develop spontaneously as countries grow richer, but this approach significantly underestimates the politics involved in the process of market development (see Robison, 2006). The developmental state literature is devoted primarily to the politics of resource mobilisation and with regard to finance, its focus is primarily directed to considering how national bureaucratic and political elites have intervened in the allocation of credit to specific sectors and interests. The idea of the entrepreneurial state differs from this conception by focusing upon market creation and development through the prism of institutional innovations that are encouraged and facilitated by states. The entrepreneurial state assumes the role of market builder by constructing quasi-market institutions that do things that elsewhere are left to private institutions. At the same time, it operates under different conditions from the "repressed" financial systems typically associated with developmental states (McKinnon, 1973).

In this article we explore three mechanisms of state-led market innovation in capital markets: national or local (as opposed to the US-based global) credit rating agencies; mortgage corporations; and bond pricing agencies. National credit rating agencies rate the creditworthiness of debt in local currency, whereas mortgage corporations create markets in securitised housing loans. Bond pricing agencies, for their part, put a value on illiquid debt instruments to enable mark-to-market portfolio management – i.e. the valuation of portfolios at current market prices rather than on some other basis, such as historical cost. Together these three mechanisms constitute the core elements of what are usually seen as the key determinants of a financial market (demand for creditworthy products; supply of tradeable assets; and the fixing of a price to those assets). These mechanisms influence the nature of market operations by producing outcomes that differ markedly from the ideal type represented by the free market.

Financial instruments such as bonds are not merely tools of convenience. They are crucial determinants of the organisational shape and governance structure of financial systems and of the specific character of credit practices. The shift from a bank-based financial system to a system of capital market finance and the growing importance of bond finance are significant elements of contemporary socioeconomic change that warrant explanation. They are tied up intimately with the ongoing reconfiguration of Asian political economies and of state-market relations more generally. Progressive financial disintermediation has been one of the most significant transformations of the world economy over the last two decades (see also Rethel and Sinclair, 2012). It has played a significant part in the "financialisation" of Asian capitalisms, understood here as the growing influence of capital markets over economic, political and social life (Pike and Pollard, 2010).

As well as looking at mechanisms of bond market development in emerging East Asian economies, we want to engage with the literature on financialisation. We regard this as imperative for at least two reasons. First, while the global credit crunch has highlighted the predicaments created by the ongoing financialisation of Anglo-American capitalism, little is known about the causes and consequences of financialisation outside the Anglo-American core. Indeed, the nascent financialisation literature is heavily biased towards the study of advanced capitalisms and here again largely restricted to analyses of "liberal market economies" (Rethel, 2010b, pp. 461–62; Krippner, 2005; Langley, 2008; Montgomerie, 2008; cf. Hall and Soskice, 2001). This paper attempts to remedy this shortcoming by looking at processes of financialisation in East Asia.

Second, apart from this geographical bias in the literature, there is also a lack of research on the regional dimension of financialisation. So far, studies of financialisation have focused either on its global dimension (in so doing often equating "global" with "American"; see, for example, the contributions in Epstein, 2005) or have looked at largely domestic processes of financialisation, emphasising the "everyday politics" of finance (Seabrooke, 2006; Langley, 2008). Little is known about the regional drivers of financialisation. We suggest that there is a distinct regional dimension to recent processes of financialisation in Asia, especially if we look at initiatives to develop and promote debt securities or bond markets. By comparing efforts to develop bond markets in the countries of this region, this article identifies the increasingly hybrid forms of state-market interaction that underpin financialisation.

Our argument is organised as follows. The next section will discuss some of the core features of bond finance. The subsequent discussion contrasts our concept of the entrepreneurial state with traditional conceptualisations of the developmental state. Having thus laid the conceptual groundwork of this paper, we turn to exploring the development of bond markets as a site of state transformation. The final section highlights some of our principal insights.

Why Bond Markets Matter

Bonds are debt certificates specifying the relationship between creditor and debtor. They state the sum lent and the debtor's obligation towards the creditor. Bonds are often referred to as securities, debentures or obligations. What distinguishes bond debt from the other major form of debt provided by the financial system – bank loans – is that bonds are easily transferable between market participants. Through bonds a loan is broken up into smaller denominations and usually these claims are marketable, meaning that they can be bought and sold in a secondary market. As a consequence bonds are more liquid than traditional bank loans. They are a very "mobile" form of capital (Watson, 2007; Watson, 1999; Sinclair and Thomas, 2001; Chwieroth and Sinclair, 2013). This mobility has implications for the role of bond finance as a *mode* of financing – i.e. the way credit is created and allocated. The increasingly important role of bond markets as a source of funds coincides with the more general paradigm shift from bank-intermediated finance to disintermediated market finance. This shift is more pervasive than commonly perceived and a series of emerging East Asian economies have succumbed to this trend, as we show below.

Bonds are used – and bond markets are developed – to mobilise credit. The development of the financial system influences and is in turn influenced by the extent to which money is "borrowable" or has liquidity. By increasing the number of instruments through which money can be saved, such as bonds, a larger volume of savings can be mobilised. Importantly, liquidity affects who has access to credit and at what price, so within existing financial structures the effects of increased liquidity are rarely neutral. Liquidity can exacerbate the uneven distribution of financial resources, making credit more easily obtained, in larger amounts and at cheaper rates for some, but effectively excluding others (Leyshon and Thrift, 1997). In other words, there is a systemic component to the allocation of credit, which is ignored by the equilibrium models of mainstream economics. Given this, we argue that more attention needs to be paid to the institutional arrangements that determine access to credit and within which efforts to expand bond markets are undertaken.

In a bank-based financial system, credit is intermediated by banks. No direct relationship exists between lenders and borrowers as banks act as "go-betweens", assuming risk. They take deposits and make loans. In addition, they screen applicants for loans and monitor loans once extended. In this ideal-typical scenario, bank income is the difference between the interest paid to depositors and that received from lenders. Indeed, as profit-making enterprises, banks are "more than neutral 'go-betweens'" (Palazzo and Rethel, 2008, p. 195). Often, but not always, the relationship between bank and borrower is based on long-term considerations, an arrangement sometimes termed "relational capitalism", whereas capital markets tend to be characterised by a synchronic logic of short-term profit maximisation (Dezalay and Garth, 1997; see also Sinclair, 2005; Harmes, 1998). The shift from a bank-intermediated financial system to a system of disintermediated market finance does not make banks superfluous, but it fundamentally changes their role (Hardie and Howarth, 2011; Rethel and Sinclair, 2012). Essentially, banks remain banks only in name. Interest income is downgraded as a feature of their balance sheets. Instead, banks derive their income from fees for underwriting, consultancy and other activities, which changes the incentive structure under which they operate, contributing to a more short-term orientation to their business (Ertürk and Solari, 2007). Commercial or corporate banking becomes relatively less important in proportion to investment banking. Relational capitalism is replaced by "arm's-length" capitalism and more selective bank-borrower relationships (Rajan, 1992; Zysman, 1983). In the process, the shift towards disintermediated finance affects access to and distribution of financial resources.

Bond finance changes not only the quantity of funds available, but also how funds are redistributed between borrowers, lenders and intermediaries. It affects power relationships in finance and the allocation of credit. This is because raising capital via bond issuance is only economically rational for companies that have achieved a certain size. Similarly, reputation is crucial in arm's-length markets such as bond markets, which privileges firms with a good credit history. Overall, bond financing is favourable to big, long-established companies, but costly and more difficult to obtain for smaller and younger entities (thus, for example, the higher interest rates on so-called junk bonds in the Western world and the absence of this type of financial instrument in many Asian economies). Creditworthiness, narrowly defined as debt repayment capacity, emerges as a central issue. In a world of capital market-oriented finance, the screening and monitoring of loans is no longer a responsibility of banks but is that of investors and institutions operating on investors' behalf such as credit rating agencies (Sinclair, 2005; 1994a; 1994b). An important consequence of this is that investment assessment and decisions are separated. The assessment, however, remains centralised in that the nodal point for information and judgment-making is often only a handful of organisations. For example, there exist only two or three internationally renowned bond rating agencies, Standard & Poor's and Moody's (and perhaps Fitch). Nevertheless, recent years have also witnessed the emergence of a growing number of national credit rating agencies (NCRAs) which is a trend that we will discuss in relation to emerging East Asia later in the article.

Modern finance theory generally assumes that the development of bond markets helps to diversify risk by broadening the range of assets for investment. Bond finance provides the basis for securitisation. Securitisation is a process in which loans, or more specifically the future cash flows to be generated from these loans, are pooled and sold on in the form of bonds. These loans can be of various origins – for example, mortgages, or consumer loans for cars, or credit card receivables. Securitisation effectively converts real assets and claims into liquid financial claims. The effects of securitisation are pervasive. By selling on loans, banks can take them off their balance sheets and thus, it is thought, reduce their risk exposure. Moreover, by releasing capital, securitisation also enhances liquidity, assuming market participants have confidence in the securitised assets. In theory, securitisation aids the diversification of risk and could thus potentially lead to a more stable financial system (CGFS, 2007; 2003). Yet in practice, due to the separation of the origination and the holding of risk, securitisation has tended to increase risk, as demonstrated in the global financial crisis that began in 2007 (Best, 2010; De Goede, 2004). Securitisation techniques have nevertheless become increasingly widespread, not only in those countries most affected by the global financial crisis, but also in emerging East Asia.

While in a bank-intermediated financial system decisions about the allocation of credit are centralised in the hands of a few banks, in a securitised economy they are, *prima facie*, made by a larger group of individual and institutional investors that purchase and hold or trade small denominated debt certificates. The tradeability of bonds does not, however, mean that bond markets come close to the atomised structure posited by the ideal type market model of mainstream economics. Investment decisions are to a large extent in the hands of unit trusts or mutual funds and other institutional investors. These are often buy-and-hold investors with little interest in trading, which can make it difficult to obtain up-to-date market valuations of bond prices. This has become quite a challenge over the last decade as mark-to-market accounting, where valuations are meant to reflect current market prices, has become more widely adopted (Perry and Nölke, 2006). Especially in countries where bond markets are still relatively young or dominated by just a few big investors, obtaining current market valuations for illiquid bond assets can pose significant problems. This also holds true for some of the East Asian bond markets we discuss below.

Credit ratings, securitisation techniques and pricing mechanisms are important aspects of bond market development. They also have an inherently political nature. Financing methods, and the importance attributed to them within specific financial systems, are at the core of the everyday reproduction of financial orders (Seabrooke, 2006). Above all, bond finance creates an "economy of obligation" as the economic historian Craig Muldrew (1998) has argued. The development of bond markets both induces and is premised on qualitative and institutional changes in the working of the state and its agencies in relation to both the financial system and the wider political economy. As we will outline in the following sections, more attention must be paid to the constitutive role of the state in making these markets. Bond finance and bond markets matter. The development of bond markets affects how savings are mobilised; it affects the principles according to which credit is allocated (and thus influences who has access to credit and at what price); it manipulates the distribution of risk and reward; and it can act as a source of both discipline and leverage.

From Developmental State to Entrepreneurial State

There are many competing views about what defines the developmental state (Stubbs, 2009, p. 9). At the core of most accounts is a strong administrative capability (such as Japan's Ministry of International Trade and Industry, examined by Chalmers Johnson [1982], weak civil society institutions, and a context of external threats and support (the Cold War and alliance with the United States). The mobilisation of capital is usually seen as a core feature of the developmental state model. This dimension of the developmental state sought to regulate investment much like the rules of the road regulate driving. The capital needs of both households and small enterprises were seen as subordinate to the overarching goal of achieving national economic growth. Finance was subordinated to the needs of the "real", industrial economy and designed to serve industrial strategy.

As Wade (2004, p. 27) points out, a key feature of the developmental state was its control over the financial system, "making private financial capital subordinate to industrial capital". Yet, state control of the financial sector was also used to further other socioeconomic goals such as, for example in the case of Malaysia, the indigenisation of the financial system and the redistribution of corporate ownership along ethnic lines. According to advocates of the developmental state model, short-term market logic would not generate the long-term investment necessary for industrialisation. Instead, they advocated a system in which government "encouraged" investment in targeted sectors and segments of the economy that government identified as crucial for economic transformation (Amsden, 1989). Some, however, argued further that the state was not only reallocating financial resources from one thing to another, but could also mobilise new funds and stimulate investment (Wade, 2004). Nevertheless, the allocation of credit was geared towards big business, which was already well placed to generate funds internally. Risk was very concentrated, which made this model of "indebted industrialisation" highly vulnerable to shocks (Bowie and Unger, 1997, p. 13; see also Wade and Veneroso, 1998), so it relied on a certain degree of insulation from the world economy (e.g. through capital controls and restrictions). Moreover, as state development planning agencies monitored industries and made overall investment decisions, banks had only a limited disciplinary function over business activity.

The transition to a disintermediated system of market finance provides fundamental challenges to this developmental state model. As the emerging East Asian economies became increasingly integrated with the world economy, it was more difficult to afford the insulation necessary to maintain the developmental state system of old. Similarly, capital markets increasingly competed with banks as the main source of funding. We argue that since the Asian financial crisis the state form characteristic of emerging East Asia has shifted substantially from the developmental state to what we call the entrepreneurial state. Given the changed context the strategy of "picking winners" is no longer dynamic enough for a world in which technologies and financial innovations are rapidly introduced and seemingly just as rapidly become obsolete. Nor is the developed world neoliberal state form that merely seeks to create the right conditions for innovation attractive in the context of emerging East Asian challenges and ambitions. Our conception of the entrepreneurial state acknowledges that cooperation between market participants in developing new institutions and processes is often difficult. States are able to knit together large networks and encourage their cooperation. The entrepreneurial state is not simply trying to do development itself; nor is it just adapting or retreating in the face of greater market freedom.

The concept of an "entrepreneurial state" has been applied in the East Asian context before. Jane Duckett used the term to explain that the state in China became involved in the economy during the 1990s but in ways that contributed to the development of marketisation rather than reinforcing the existence of a command economy with a directive state at its core (Duckett, 1996, p. 182; 1998). For Duckett, the term "entrepreneurial state" refers to the business activities of the state, specifically at the local level. But she does not see the idea of the entrepreneurial state as a comprehensive model of the state. It does not represent an alternative concept to the developmental state for her, as it does for us (Duckett, 1996, p. 189). Duckett's entrepreneurial state is a disaggregation of the developmental state that allows for better analysis of its component parts.

Yu's examination of economic development in Singapore, Taiwan, South Korea and Hong Kong also involves the utilisation of the concept of the entrepreneurial state to further specify the developmental state model (Yu, 1997). In contrast to Duckett, what defines Yu's entrepreneurial state is not that it engages in business but that it employs a distinctive cognitive process that is a feature of its activities (Yu, 2001, p. 752). For Yu, "entrepreneurial learning" is key (Yu, 1997, p. 49). This is apparent when governments are "alert to change, and discover and exploit opportunities" (Yu, 1997, p. 51). Planning, learning and the revising of plans are characteristic of entrepreneurial states.

Pereira uses the concept of the entrepreneurial state as a label for specific behaviour by state agencies. What defines entrepreneurship is not the act of offering commercial services but the pursuit of hitherto unnoticed opportunities for profit for the enrichment of the state itself (Pereira, 2004, p. 130). When this occurs outside the confines of the home state, as in the case of the Singapore government's industrial parks in Batam and Suzhou, it raises the question of whether entrepreneurial states can be distinguished from transnational corporations.

In our conceptualisation, the entrepreneurial state is a new form of state that recognises positive dynamics such as "network effects". It is also conscious of the incentives some established companies have to be rent-seekers and obstruct change. The entrepreneurial state is focused on institutional innovation at a deeper, constitutive level, recognising the limitations of picking winners (characteristic of the developmental state) and of merely getting the environment right (the state form increasingly typical of developed countries after about 1980). The entrepreneurial state is now characteristic of emerging East Asia and nowhere is this role clearer than in the catalyst function the entrepreneurial state has served in developing bond markets in the region. In turn, the emergence of bond markets has facilitated the process of state transformation from an ideal-typical developmental to an ideal-typical entrepreneurial state. Table 1 identifies the differences between these two ideal-typical forms of state in emerging East Asia.

How does this new state form, the entrepreneurial state, actually help to bring about innovation in East Asia? We think there are at least three core mechanisms. The first of these, institutional isomorphism or structural homogeneity, encourages conformity. It refers to the encouragement of institution building on the basis of already-existing structural relationships with the US or other developed countries. DiMaggio and Powell (1983, p. 150) suggested that one way in which institutional isomorphism occurs is through normative isomorphism, especially via professional codes and norms. Civil servants and associated experts such as economists in emerging East Asia are socialised into a professional culture, often through the attainment of graduate education and work experience in developed countries. It makes sense to adopt or adapt institutions being used in the developed world for the purposes of bringing change to emerging East Asian economies. National credit rating agencies are our example of this mechanism.

Another way in which the entrepreneurial state pursues innovation is by adapting old institutions to new purposes. This is a time honoured tradition in the developed world. The International Monetary Fund started life in the 1940s as an institution intended to smooth the path to balance of payments adjustment, in order to prevent dramatic, politically unacceptable change. By the 1980s it had become an agent of precisely the sort of structural change it had been established to obviate. Using an existing institution is a potentially cheap and easy solution to new problems. Housing finance agencies and mortgage corporations are our example of this form of innovation mechanism.

The entrepreneurial state has also facilitated the creation of new institutions to deliver the sort of innovation of which we write. Yet rather than place emphasis on a rational-choice notion of how institutions come into being, as designed to maximise

Table 1. Developmental State versus Entrepreneurial State

Type of State	Developmental	Entrepreneurial
Source of Value	Industry and manufacturing	Services and the "knowledge economy"
Financial System	Bank-based	Disintermediated
Network effect	Not recognised	Central
Expertise/ knowledge	Public (policy)	Private (market)
Outcome	Controlled	Open-ended/unintended effects
Governance	Command, based on industrial model; interventionist	Encourage, based on innovation model; facilitating
Bureaucracy	Integrated, elite	Separate, creation of autonomy/ privatised institutions
Future	Certain	Uncertain

Source: The Authors.

objectives, we think a different logic fits better with at least some mechanisms of innovation in emerging East Asia. This is the logic of appropriateness, which suggests that it is deontic structures as identified by Searle (2005) that are central to how mechanisms work. This view of institutional origins suggests that such mechanisms emerge in light of prevailing norms. If there is no market, or nothing that looks like market price, then it makes sense for the emerging East Asian state to facilitate the creation of new institutions, such as bond pricing agencies, to kick-start this process.

Finance as Site of State Transformation: Mechanisms of Bond Market Development in Asia

Recent years have seen the rapid expansion of local currency bond markets in Asia (Rethel, 2010a). In the wake of the Asian financial crisis, policymakers perceived the development of regional bond markets as a way to deal with the double mismatch of short-term, dollar-denominated borrowing for long-term, local currency investments, whose flaws had become so apparent during the crisis (Katada, 2009, p. 11). In addition, developing and promoting regional bond markets is an attempt to improve the financial infrastructure to increase the retention of savings in the region, especially as the required investments for regional infrastructure development are high (see, for example, Kawai, 2006, cited in Dent, 2008, p. 775).

Indeed, as Table 2 indicates, in the East Asian economies the overall share of local bond markets as a percentage of GDP has grown dramatically over the last decade.[1] Moreover, in all countries listed except for China PRC, capital market finance (bonds and equities) is now a more significant source of funds than domestic credit institutions such as banks (Rethel and Sinclair, 2012, p. 61). Nevertheless, national variations persist. Thus, for example, in South Korea bond issuance by corporations exceeds that of the government, a trend that also held for Malaysia until increased government bond issuance occurred with the onset of the global financial crisis. In countries such as Indonesia and the Philippines domestic bond markets remain dominated by government bonds.

Table 2. Local Currency Bond Markets as Percentage of GDP, 2001 and 2011

	2001			2011		
Market	**Govt**	**Corp**	**Total**	**Govt**	**Corp**	**Total**
CN	17.7	0.3	18	33.9	11.4	45.3
HK	8.8	29.2	38	37.1	31.9	69
ID	29.8	1.1	31	11.4	2	13.4
JP	84.8	21.2	106	196.5	19.6	216.1
KR	27.3	54.2	81.5	47.5	67	114.5
MY	43.1	41.1	84.2	56.6	38	94.6
PH	33.8	0.1	33.9	30.3	4.5	34.8
SG	34.1	30.4	64.5	47	28.2	75.1
TH	25.9	4.9	30.8	54.5	13	67.5
VN	0.6	0	0.6	12.7	1.7	14.4

Key: CN: People's Republic of China; HK: Hong Kong SAR; ID: Indonesia; JP: Japan; KR: South Korea; MY: Malaysia; PH: Philippines; SG: Singapore; TH: Thailand; VN: Vietnam.
Source: ADB (2012).

In the following section, we focus on three mechanisms of bond market development: credit ratings; securitisation via mortgage corporations; and bond valuations by bond pricing agencies and similar institutions. These three institutional devices mirror the core elements of the market: demand, supply and price. Credit ratings confer bonds with creditworthiness. They thus influence the demand for this type of financial instrument. Mortgage corporations turn mortgages into debt securities and thus act as suppliers of this type of financial instrument. Bond pricing agencies provide "as if" market prices for illiquid assets. Taken together, these three types of institutional innovation – manifestations of different innovative approaches whose emergence was facilitated by the entrepreneurial state – mimic the operation of the free market, yet produce outcomes that are quite distinctive.

National credit rating agencies and institutional isomorphism

Japan was the first country in East Asia to have significant local credit rating agencies, starting in the mid-1980s. The Ministry of Finance was heavily involved in their creation, adopting the broad outlines of the existing US agencies, but few market observers saw them as independent or took them seriously for many years because the process of emulation did not initially reproduce the independence of the US agencies (Sinclair, 2005). Twenty-five years after their foundation two Japanese agencies have been recognised by the US Securities and Exchange Commission as Nationally Recognized Statistical Rating Organizations (NRSROs), like Moody's and Standard & Poor's, suggesting that these institutions have now acquired market legitimacy.

Why might emerging Asian states want their own rating agencies to encourage bond market development in Asia when they can make use of Moody's and S&P? The best explanation is that the Global Credit Rating Agencies (GCRAs) based in the US did not deem local bond markets in Asia outside Japan profitable enough, given their – at least until very recently – small scale. It was therefore up to the entrepreneurial state to take action. The experience of Malaysia in the late 1980s is instructive. Here, the impulse to set up a rating agency came from both domestic regulators and international and regional multilateral organisations such as the International Finance Corporation (IFC, part of the World Bank Group) and the Asian Development Bank (ADB). Domestic policymakers were open to linking their new domestic institutions with global networks to achieve institutional isomorphism, and favoured a model where two rating agencies were set up in Malaysia, one in cooperation with Standard & Poor's and the other with Moody's. The US-based agencies, however, had little interest in Malaysia. The Malaysian bond market was small and profits were thought too low for them to become active in the market (Nor Mohamed, 2004). In 1990 Rating Agency Malaysia Berhad (RAM) was incorporated. Its first CEO was a long-serving official from the Malaysian central bank who had additional experience in the Ministry of Finance. It was the entrepreneurial state that ensured this well-known form of market infrastructure was built. In 1995 a second rating agency, Malaysian Rating Corporation Berhad (MARC), was established. Financial policymakers thought a more competitive market for credit ratings would improve their quality and thus further contribute to a mature, fully developed and internationally competitive bond market.

By setting up national credit rating agencies, entrepreneurial states responded to a perceived gap in domestic financial infrastructure with a well-understood institutional model. In so doing, they played a constitutive role, independent of whether they were the principal shareholders or the agencies were *prima facie* privately owned. This suggests that the entrepreneurial state no longer has the post-colonial impulse toward control typical of its predecessor. That older style of politics is no longer compelling. The entrepreneurial state is much more interested in performance and achieving objectives, even if it means deploying foreign-sourced institutional solutions. National agencies may be better able to serve locally-focused investors interested in small and medium-sized enterprises (SMEs) than Moody's and S&P (ADB, 2010, p. 2). Given the smaller scale of these agencies their fees are more modest than those charged by the global majors.

From an international point of view emerging East Asian NCRAs remain relatively small and have few reputational assets compared to the GCRAs. The idea that NCRAs are inherently compromised by state involvement and financial sector ownership, as is typically the case, is perhaps a less compelling concern today given the problems with GCRAs that emerged during the global financial crisis that began in 2007. The NCRAs have mostly signed up to the IOSCO code of conduct for credit rating agencies, demonstrating a determination to improve the quality of their output and increase their reputational assets over time. The privatisation of Korea Ratings in 1999 should be seen as part of this process of authority enhancement, in which the entrepreneurial state, having done its job, is able to let the new quasi-market institution take on greater market characteristics and complete the process of institutional isomorphism.

On the regional level, there is the Association of Credit Rating Agencies Asia (ACRAA). Its 26 members include rating agencies from the East Asian region, but also from outside countries such as India, Pakistan and Bahrain (Islamic International Rating Agency). ACRAA's efforts to promote Asian bond markets are primarily targeted at generating network effects from the exchange of information and knowledge, for example through its regular "Best Practice Dialogue", and training. In addition to this initiative on the regional level, there is a crisscrossing of links between different national agencies. The willingness of states to foster regional links and, where attractive, links between NCRAs and GCRAs, suggests that the entrepreneurial state is highly flexible and adaptable. This is not the protectionist state that must have its steel factory but the state that recognises the utility of imported models. The entrepreneurial state in Asia seems to work like a (good) operating system in a computer: happy to make programs work together to serve the needs of the user.

State involvement in these agencies does not take either a developmental or neoliberal form. States are not forcing private capital to stop using banks. Nor are states sitting back and letting the market develop whatever institutions are required. Asian states have – however implicitly – recognised the benefits of network effects in promoting this system, and have set about importing a prototype of the institutions from the US. In this regard what we call the entrepreneurial state is playing a much deeper and longer-term game than the developmental state that preceded it. Network effects have a social, organic quality to them and time is clearly crucial to their development.

Mortgage corporations: Institutional isomorphism and adaptation

Government-supported housing finance agencies, tasked with providing affordable housing loans either directly to individuals or indirectly via the banking sector, have existed in the region for decades. The establishment of mortgage corporations and the introduction of advanced securitisation techniques in emerging Asian bond markets gained momentum with the Asian financial crisis. In recent years, housing finance agencies have played an increasingly important role in the development of domestic bond markets through the issuance of mortgage- and other asset-backed securities. In so doing, they have pursued "similar objectives but different approaches" (Chan et al., 2006, p. 74). Thus, for example, the Japanese Government Housing Loan Corporation and Korea Housing Finance Corporation lend directly to households, while Cagamas Berhad, the Malaysian Mortgage Corporation, and the Hong Kong Mortgage Corporation (HKMC) provide liquidity to lenders by purchasing housing loans from housing agencies such as the Malaysian Treasury Housing Loan Division and banks, but do not provide direct loans. Indeed, this points to two different strategies of institutional innovation, institutional adaptation and institutional isomorphism, which these agencies represent.

Let us deal with the latter first. In another example of state-led institutional isomorphism in emerging East Asian bond markets, Cagamas and HKMC, both established before the outbreak of the Asian financial crisis, are modelled on the US mortgage agency, Fannie Mae. Cagamas' biggest shareholder – with 20 per cent – is Malaysia's central bank. Set up in the wake of the 1985–86 economic crisis primarily to provide mortgage lenders with liquidity and thus indirectly to contribute to the provision of housing, Cagamas' aims with regard to the development of the bond market were twofold. On the one hand, it was thought that by setting a precedent, Cagamas would kick-start the development of the corporate bond market. On the other hand, it functioned as a test case to try out mechanisms for the liberalisation of the government bond market (BNM, 1999). HKMC, fully owned by the Hong Kong government through its Exchange Fund, was set up in March 1997 to develop the secondary mortgage market (Lamoreaux, 1998).

In connection with the subprime crisis, the US mortgage agencies, and the securitisation strategies they promoted, have drawn a lot of attention and criticism. So it is important to highlight the differences in Cagamas' and HKMC's original operating procedures. The early Cagamas bonds were different from typical mortgage-backed securitisation instruments. Cagamas bought housing loans with recourse to the primary lender, therefore not taking on the credit risk, at least for the time being (Cagamas, 2006, p. 16). HKMC, unlike Fannie Mae, does not assist in originating mortgages (Yam, 2008). As in the case of NCRAs, it is impossible to see the creation of Cagamas as the straightforward outcome of either neoliberal- or developmental-type state efforts. At the time of its creation, the Malaysian bond market was in its infancy. Domestic credit rating agencies did not exist and, in the absence of a corporate bond market, the only available price indicators derived from a non-competitive government securities market in which bonds were held by captive lenders. In this context, Cagamas played an important role by broadening the pool of investable bond assets. Similarly, through HKMC, the Hong Kong Monetary Authority was trying to alleviate pressures on bank balance sheets.

When it comes to pioneering and promoting securitisation techniques in the region, however, dynamics of institutional adaptation must not be ignored. Indeed, there has been a significant shift in the objectives of many housing finance agencies away from primarily providing liquidity to mortgage markets towards securitising a whole range of assets. Over the last decade or so, these agencies have continuously broadened their range of activities, with regard to both underlying assets and the capital market instruments they issue. In this regard, securitisation has become an increasingly important part of their business. For example, Cagamas conducted its first full securitisation transaction in 1999 and began to securitise credit card receivables in 2003 and SME loans in 2007. KHFC started to securitise student loans in 2005. Financial innovation in the form of securitisation and the resulting increased interdependence of banking and capital market practices is perhaps the most important change that has occurred with regard to the supply side of capital markets in Asia over the last decade. Again, state involvement in these agencies does not take either a developmental or neoliberal form, but is a clear manifestation of the entrepreneurial state and the increasingly hybrid state-market interactions that underpin it.

New institutions: Bond pricing agencies

The Asian financial crisis exposed the lack of transparency in financial markets. In its wake, several Asian political economies shifted to the use of so-called "fair value" or "mark-to-market" accounting for portfolio valuations (Walter, 2008; see Perry and Nölke, 2006 for a critical discussion of this practice). With regard to bond investments this posed a problem in that many bonds are traded over-the-counter and not on a daily basis, which proved problematic when it came to obtaining the daily market prices of these bonds. In response to this, an important new set of institutions emerged – so-called Bond Pricing Agencies (BPAs). BPAs are an important means for the price finding process in less liquid domestic bond markets. They develop models that help to assign a price to debt securities, especially in cases where little trading occurs and daily quotations are absent.

The first East Asian BPAs were created in Korea in 2000. This followed a decision in November 1997, at the height of Korea's crisis, to introduce mark-to-market accounting and subsequent efforts to introduce bond valuation systems by the Korean government. The three Korean BPAs, Korea Bond Pricing, KIS Pricing and NICE Pricing, are all spin-offs from Korea's biggest three NCRAs. In this case, the involvement of the state has been more that of an indirect facilitator. Thailand introduced bond valuations following the 2005 change of the Thai Bond Dealing Center into the Thai Bond Market Association (ThaiBMA), a self-regulatory organisation approved by the Securities and Exchange Commission Thailand. Membership in the ThaiBMA is mandatory for bond market participants such as dealers, who have to comply with ThaiBMA regulations. Part of ThaiBMA's mandate is to provide "rational pricing" for weakly traded bonds (World Bank, 2006, p. 34). In both cases, the government played a facilitating role by creating the necessary regulatory framework, which made the emergence of these institutions near-imperative.

In both Malaysia and Indonesia the government played a more proactive role in the creation of BPAs. Here, the emergence of BPAs was closely tied to financial development planning. Bond Pricing Agency Malaysia (BPAM) was created in 2004 on the initiative of the Malaysian Securities Commission, which for this purpose released guidelines to "facilitate the introduction of bond pricing agencies" (SC, 2006). Enabling mark-to-market pricing was deemed important to facilitate the growth of Malaysia's private unit trust industry. While BPAM was established as a private company, Indonesia

Bond Pricing Agency is a "government-created" company, in that its shareholders are the three key Indonesian capital market bodies – the Indonesia Stock Exchange, the Indonesian Central Securities Depository and the Indonesian Stock Market Clearing House (Aditya, 2008). It was the result of a long planning process that began in 2005, but only led to the creation of IBPA in 2008.

With regard to BPAs, similar network effects are at play as in the cases of NCRAs and mortgage corporations. While BPAM was set up on the initiative of the Malaysian Securities Commission, it recruited staff from Malaysia's two rating agencies, as well as market practitioners and regulatory officials, but there is also a regional dimension to these network effects. Mainstream & Co., the company partnered with Korea Bond Pricing, helped to create BPAM. Indeed, with a stake of 20 per cent each, Rating Agency Malaysia and Mainstream & Co. used to be BPAM's biggest shareholders (Yong, 2006). A similar set up was intended for Indonesia Bond Pricing Agency in that BPAM was to provide technical assistance to IBPA, but in the end cooperation between BPAM and IBPA was called off. These BPAs are a clear product of the entrepreneurial state. What their evolution in East Asia suggests is that even on this level, there is not only increased interdependence (contributing to the network effects discussed earlier once the ball got rolling), but deliberate institution-building to further the promotion and development of Asian bond markets.

In the wake of the Asian financial crisis of 1997–98, governments in the region decided that markets had to become more transparent to create trust in these markets and to confer credibility on them. For this purpose, setting up BPAs was an important institutional device, but in so doing the idea of the free market, where the price is determined by the intersection of demand and supply, is put aside. By assigning daily "as if" market prices to the bonds they value, often illiquid securities not traded on a daily basis, BPAs turn the price discovery mechanism propagated by mainstream economics on its head (see also Watson, 2005). Nevertheless, the developmental state model cannot account for this dynamic either. Prices are not gotten deliberately wrong as suggested by Amsden to channel economic activity where the government wants it. Indeed, BPAs are tasked with discovering a bond's "true" value (or at least approximating it as closely as possible) to facilitate an efficient, market-based allocation of capital.

In sum, the three major institutional innovations in Asian capital markets introduced within the last two and a half decades – credit ratings, mortgage corporations and bond pricing agencies – cannot straightforwardly be characterised as market mechanisms. Their emergence was not spontaneous to address a functional gap as mainstream economics would make us believe, but by design. Yet neither were they established by command to effect a controlled outcome. It is the open-endedness of this process that will allow them to grapple with the uncertain future that globalised capital markets hold. In this development, the state maintained an important gatekeeper function, serving as conduit for the creation, absorption and ultimately institutionalisation of market knowledge in the domestic financial system.

Conclusion: Why Bond Market Development Matters

We conclude by highlighting some of the key dilemmas faced by the entrepreneurial state in emerging East Asia that come into sharp relief through the lens of bond market development examined in this article. While entrepreneurial states in emerging East

Asia do not seek control of outcomes in the specific sense of volume of steel production or automobiles exported in a given year, they do care about moving up the value chain and improving and maintaining the international competitiveness of their country. But this long-term commitment on the part of entrepreneurial states, albeit realised in innovative forms, runs counter to the short-termist logic of financialisation that has dominated global finance for the past two decades, including in emerging East Asia to a degree. One of the most remarkable aspects of this transition is that it has attracted little attention, let alone political contestation in the region. We think that this is partly due to the rather technical character of bond markets, a notion that we have sought to unpack in section 2 of this article, by highlighting their political and social significance. Moreover, many of the changes in the operation of financial systems that we have discussed here are only indirectly felt by the concerned populations, for example in the form of rising levels of household debt. Even here, developments such as significant personal debt crises in South Korea and Taiwan in the early 2000s and rapidly rising house prices in countries such as Malaysia and Singapore, fuelled by a finance-led growth strategy, have – so far – given rise to little overt resistance.

There are striking similarities between the organisational premises of disintermediated capital markets and the entrepreneurial state form in emerging East Asia. Both are organised on an arm's length basis as networks of institutions. This pattern can be contrasted with the developmental state and bank-based finance, both of which are hierarchical command-and-control structures. Although there are many adaptive features to the entrepreneurial state and capital markets, they are not about codified, long-term relationships. The relationships in both cases are more contingent. This does not mean they are inevitably short-termist. If production remains central to emerging East Asia, and financialisation does not dominate to the extent it has come to in the developed world, the link between the entrepreneurial state form and disintermediated capital markets could be profoundly innovative and transformative.

The new state form we have identified is fundamental to the success of the emerging capital market system in East Asia. This of course takes different trajectories in different countries, and nuances of this process abound. The market mechanism is characterised by allocation through price, not plan. Yet, how does one find the price of what Polanyi calls a "fictitious commodity" such as capital, and bonds in particular? In contrast to tangible goods markets, in capital markets future cash streams are traded. Prices thus depend on credibility and transparency, but most of all on trust. The entrepreneurial state plays a constitutive role in this regard, and efforts to increase the transparency of the capital market have to be interpreted accordingly.

In terms of how the concept of the entrepreneurial state can be developed further, we think more attention should be paid to how specific policy knowledge is created within the entrepreneurial state (e.g. through mechanisms of institutional isomorphism, adaptation and invention), how it recombines with other forms of knowledge (e.g. through processes of internationalisation, diffusion and socialisation), and how it translates into institutional change. There is a broad consensus in emerging East Asia between state and market players when it comes to the perceived necessity and benefits of the promotion of bond markets. Nevertheless, national variations in the specific characteristics of the entrepreneurial state exist when it comes to development of domestic local currency bond markets.

Progressive financial disintermediation, especially the expansion of bond finance, has significantly affected financial culture in emerging East Asia and induced a wide range of behavioural changes with regard to both state and market actors. Its socioeconomic implications are pervasive, ranging from the emergence of a new politics of debt to a decisive shift in individual financial habits. Changing credit practices, which were underwritten by entrepreneurial states in emerging East Asia, have in turn been a necessary condition for the transformation of bank-intermediated financial systems into disintermediated systems of market finance, which has contributed to the consolidation of the entrepreneurial state model in the region.

Note

1. The exception in this data set is Indonesia, where the size of the domestic bond market has actually shrunk between 2001 and 2011. In 1997, the first year for which this data set contains a figure for Indonesia, its market size was only 2.4 per cent of GDP and a subsequent increase in government bond issuance was largely due to Indonesia's financial restructuring in the aftermath of the global financial crisis.

References

ADB (2012) AsianBondsOnline – Size of LCY bond market in % of GDP. Available at http://asianbondsonline.adb.org/regional/data/bondmarket.php?code=LCY_in_GDP_Local, accessed 11 December 2012.

ADB (2010) *Best practice for regulatory framework and use of credit rating information of domestic credit rating agencies in South Asia* (Manila: Asian Development Bank).

Aditya Wikrama (2008) New bond pricing agency poised to start work. The Jakarta Global, 8 November. Available at http://www.thejakartaglobe.com/business/new-bond-pricing-agency-poised-to-start-work/299930#Scene_1, accessed 10 October 2012.

Amsden, Alice (1989) *Asia's next giant: South Korea and late industrialization* (Oxford: Oxford University Press).

Best, Jacqueline (2010) The limits of financial risk management: The subprime crisis in critical perspective. *New Political Economy* 15(3), pp. 29–49.

BNM (1999) *The Central Bank and the financial system in Malaysia. A decade of change, 1989–1999* (Kuala Lumpur: Bank Negara Malaysia).

Bowie, Alasdair and Danny Unger (1997) *The politics of open economies: Indonesia, Malaysia, the Philippines, and Thailand* (Cambridge: Cambridge University Press).

Cagamas Berhad (2006) A study of mortgage-backed securities market in Malaysia: Cagamas' experience in developing mortgage-backed securities, in Ismail Dalla (ed.), *East Asian finance: Selected issues* (Washington, DC: World Bank).

Chan, Eric, Michael Davies and Jacob Gyntelberg (2006) The role of government-supported housing finance agencies in Asia. *BIS Quarterly Review*, December, pp. 71–83.

Chwieroth, Jeffrey M. and Timothy J. Sinclair (2013) How you stand depends on how we see: International capital mobility as social fact. *Review of International Political Economy* 20(3), pp. 457–85.

CGFS (2007) Financial stability and local currency bond markets. CGFS Publications No. 28. Available at http://www.bis.org/publ/cgfs28.htm, accessed 8 May 2008.

CGFS (2003) Credit risk transfer. CGFS Publications No. 20. Available at http://www.bis.org/publ/cgfs20.htm, accessed 6 May 2008.

De Goede, Marieke (2004) Repoliticizing financial risk. *Economy and Society* 33(2), pp. 197–217.

Dent, Christopher (2008) The Asian Development Bank and developmental regionalism in East Asia. *Third World Quarterly* 29(4), pp. 767–86.

Dezalay, Yves and Bryant Garth (1997) Law, lawyers and social capital: 'Rule of Law' versus relational capitalism. *Social & Legal Studies* 6(1), pp. 109–41.

DiMaggio, Paul J. and Walter W. Powell (1983) The iron cage revisited: Institutional isomorphism and collective rationality in organisational fields. *American Sociological Review* 48(2), pp. 147–60.

Duckett, Jane (1998) *The entrepreneurial state in China: Real estate and commerce departments in reform era Tianjin* (London: Routledge).

Duckett, Jane (1996) The emergence of the entrepreneurial state in contemporary China. *The Pacific Review* 9(2), pp. 180–98.

Epstein, Gerald, ed. (2005) *Financialisation and the world economy* (Cheltenham: Edward Elgar).

Ertürk, Ismail and Stefano Solari (2007) Banks as continuous reinvention. *New Political Economy* 12(3), pp. 369–88.

Hall, Peter A. and David Soskice, eds. (2001) *Varieties of capitalism* (Oxford: Oxford University Press).

Hameiri, Shahar (2012) Theorising regions through changes in statehood: Rethinking the theory and method of comparative regionalism. *Review of International Studies*. Available via iFirst.

Harmes, Adam (1998) Institutional investors and the reproduction of neoliberalism. *Review of International Political Economy* 5(1), pp. 92–121.

Hardie, Iain and David Howarth (2011) Market-based banking and the financial crisis. Working Paper, University of Edinburgh, Scotland. Available at http://www.pol.ed.ac.uk/__data/assets/pdf_file/0004/64561/HardieHowarthMMBFinal32011.pdf, accessed 1 June 2012.

Johnson, Chalmers A. (1982) *MITI and the Japanese miracle. The growth of industrial policy, 1925–1975* (Stanford: Stanford University Press).

Katada, Saori (2009) Political economy of East Asian integration and cooperation. Asian Development Bank Institute (ADBI) Working Paper No. 170. Available at http://www.adbi.org/files/2009.11.30.wp170.political.economy.east.asia.pdf, accessed 1 June 2012.

Krippner, Greta R. (2005) The financialization of the American economy. *Socio-Economic Review* 3(2), pp. 173–208.

Lamoreaux, Pamela (1998) A busy year for the Hong Kong Mortgage Corporation. *Housing Finance International* 13(1), pp. 33–42.

Langley, Paul (2008) *The everyday life of global finance. Saving and borrowing in Anglo-America* (Oxford: Oxford University Press).

Leyshon, Andrew and Nigel Thrift (1997) *Money/Space: Geographies of monetary transformation* (London: Routledge).

McKinnon, Ronald I. (1973) *Money and capitalism in economic development* (Washington, DC: Brookings Institution).

Montgomerie, Johnna (2008) Bridging the critical divide: Global finance, financialisation and contemporary capitalism. *Contemporary Politics* 14(3), pp. 233–52.

Muldrew, Craig (1998) *The economy of obligation: The culture of credit and social relations in early modern England* (New York: St Martin's Press).

Nor Mohamed Yakcop (2004) Special address by YB Tan Sri Dato Nor Mohamed Yakcop Second Finance Minister of Malaysia. Kuala Lumpur, 24 June. Available at http://www.treasury.gov.my/index.php?ch=36&pg=126&ac=377&lang=eng, accessed 11 May 2008.

Öniş, Ziya (1991) The logic of the developmental state. *Comparative Politics* 24(1), pp. 109–26.

Palazzo, Guido and Lena Rethel (2008) Conflicts of interest in financial intermediation. *Journal of Business Ethics* 81(1), pp. 193–207.

Pereira, Alexius A. (2004) State entrepreneurship and regional development: Singapore's industrial parks in Batam and Suzhou. *Entrepreneurship & Regional Development* 16(1), pp. 129–44.

Perry, James and Andreas Nölke (2006) The political economy of international accounting standards. *Review of International Political Economy* 13(4), pp. 559–86.

Pike, Andy and Jane Pollard (2010) Economic geographies of financialisation. *Economic Geography* 86(1), pp. 29–51.

Rajan, Raghuram G. (1992) Insiders and outsiders: The choice between informed and arm's-length debt. *Journal of Finance* 47(4), pp. 1367–400.

Rethel, Lena (2010a) The new financial development paradigm and Asian bond markets. *New Political Economy* 15(4), pp. 493–517.

Rethel, Lena (2010b) Financialisation and the Malaysian political economy. *Globalizations* 7(4), pp. 489–506.

Rethel, Lena and Timothy J. Sinclair (2012) *The problem with banks* (London: Zed Books).

Robison, Richard, ed. (2006) *The neo-liberal revolution: Forging the market state* (Basingstoke: Palgrave Macmillan).

SC (2006) New SC measures to strengthen corporate bond market – greater investor protection through enhanced price transparency and professional standards. Available at http://www.sc.com.my/main.asp?pageid=379&linkid=700&yearno=2006&mod=paper, accessed 1 May 2012.

Seabrooke, Leonard (2006) *The social sources of financial power* (Ithaca and London: Cornell University Press).

Searle, John R. (2005) What is an institution? *Journal of Institutional Economics* 1(1), pp. 1–22.

Sinclair, Timothy J. (2005) *The new masters of capital: American bond rating agencies and the politics of creditworthiness* (Ithaca: Cornell University Press).

Sinclair, Timothy J. (1994a) Passing judgement: Credit rating processes as regulatory mechanisms of governance in the emerging World Order. *Review of International Political Economy* 1(1), pp. 133–59.

Sinclair, Timothy J. (1994b) Between state and market: Hegemony and institutions of collective action under conditions of international capital mobility. *Policy Sciences* 27(4), pp. 447–66.

Sinclair, Timothy J. and Kenneth P. Thomas, eds. (2001) *Structure and agency in international capital mobility* (London and New York: Palgrave Macmillan).

Stubbs, Richard (2009) Whatever happened to the East Asian developmental state? The unfolding debate. *Pacific Review* 22(1), pp. 1–22.

Wade, Robert (2004) *Governing the market. Economic theory and the role of government in East Asian industrialization*, 2nd edition (Princeton: Princeton University Press).

Wade, Robert and Frank Veneroso (1998) The Asian crisis: The high-debt model versus the Wall Street-Treasury-IMF complex. *New Left Review* I(228), pp. 3–23.

Walter, Andrew (2008) *Governing finance. East Asia's adoption of international standards* (Ithaca: Cornell University Press).

Watson, Matthew (2007) *The political economy of international capital mobility* (Basingstoke: Palgrave Macmillan).

Watson, Matthew (2005) What makes a market economy? Schumpeter, Smith and Walras on the coordination problem. *New Political Economy* 10(2), pp. 143–61.

Watson, Matthew (1999) Rethinking capital mobility, re-regulating financial markets. *New Political Economy* 4(1), pp. 55–75.

World Bank (2006) Thailand: Country Development Partnership: Financial and Corporate Sector Competitiveness Program Assessment and Completion Report, June. Available at http://www-wds.worldbank.org/external/default/WDSContentServer/WDSP/IB/2006/09/11/000090341_20060911154624/Rendered/PDF/372810TH0P09691July071200601PUBLIC1.pdf, accessed 1 June 2012.

Yam, Joseph (2008) Viewpoint: The Hong Kong Mortgage Corporation. Hong Kong Monetary Authority, 11 September. Available at http://www.hkma.gov.hk/eng/publications-and-research/reference-materials/viewpoint/20080911.shtml, accessed 1 June 2010.

Yong, D. (2006) Bondweb wins licence to start bond valuation agency in Malaysia. Bloomberg, 8 May. Available at http://www.google.co.uk/url?sa=t&rct=j&q=rating%20agency%20malaysia%20and%20mainstream%20%26%20co&source=web&cd=4&ved=0CDUQFjAD&url=http%3A%2F%2Fwww.bondweb.com.my%2Finc%2FfileDownload_1.asp%3Ffile_loc%3D%2Fothers%2Fin_the_press%2F%26file_name%3DBloomberg060508.pdf%26Size%3D0&ei=85F1ULKQBIOc0QWKhIDADg&usg=AFQjCNGmrBXSWX-hb63vMhmEDIGJk7FGHA, accessed 10 October 2012.

Yu, Tony Fu-Lai (2001) Towards a theory of the entrepreneurial state. *International Journal of Social Economics* 28(9), pp. 752–66.

Yu, Tony Fu-Lai (1997) Entrepreneurial state: The role of government in the economic development of the Asian Newly Industrialising Economies. *Development Policy Review* 15(1), pp. 47–64.

Zysman, John (1983) *Governments, markets and growth. Financial systems and the politics of industrial change* (Ithaca and London: Cornell University Press).

Building a Venture Capital Market in Vietnam: Diffusion of a Neoliberal Market Strategy to a Socialist State

ROBYN KLINGLER-VIDRA

London School of Economics and Political Science

Abstract: *Vietnam's venture capital (VC) industry took shape in the late 1990s during a period of exceptional economic growth in the country and the development of its high-technology sector. High growth rates and technological advances have typically coincided with both strong VC market activity and state support of equity financing. This, however, has not been the case in Vietnam. In this article a policy diffusion framework is used to investigate the international and domestic origins of Vietnam's nascent VC policies, and how they became part of the agenda of the Communist Party of Vietnam (CPV) as credit-based, rather than equity-based, solutions. The article argues that Vietnam's heterodox approach to VC policy results from both external forces from donors and from domestic factors. In particular, Vietnamese policymakers have a preference for credit-based SME financing solutions and Vietnam's official development assistance providers diffuse expertise on loans, not equity investments, to the Socialist Republic. The only donors recommending VC and equity-based financing in Vietnam have gone "around the state" rather than through it by working directly with the private sector. As a result, Vietnam's SME financing initiatives have significantly diverged from international VC policy patterns.*

The conditions are right for Vietnam to be the "next China" for technology venture capital investors.

Patrick McGovern, IDG Ventures Founder and Chairman, in Fannin (2011, p. 67)

Introduction

Over the last twenty years Vietnam's economic trajectory has trended unequivocally upward. The Socialist Republic has balanced liberalisation and increased international participation with the maintenance of central planning and capital controls in what the Communist Party of Vietnam (CPV) calls a "Socialist market economy". Vietnam's growth rate has averaged more than 7 per cent annually since the 1990s, placing it in the same league as China and India as one of the world's exceptional growth stories. Analysts are equally optimistic about Vietnam's economic future. To this end, in 2010 the Economist Intelligence Unit ranked Vietnam as the world's number two emerging market for investment opportunities, second only to China. The continued excitement about investing in Vietnam comes as its private sector grows, its middle class develops, foreign direct investment (FDI) increases, and the competitiveness of its technology sector advances (Nguyen, 2007). Although Vietnam retains its agrarian prowess as the world's second largest exporter of both rice and coffee, its information and communications technology market (ICT) has been attracting international attention. ICT-sector FDI in Vietnam has grown over the last decade, as more than a dozen multinationals (MNCs), including Samsung, Nokia and Hewlett Packard, have opened factories to manufacture mobile phones, computer components and other technology goods (Hung, 2011). These are not insignificant facilities for the MNCs either; Intel Corporation's largest plant globally – which opened in 2010 – is a USD 1 billion facility near Ho Chi Minh City, in the south of the country.

In stark contrast to this technology sector growth and the broader exuberance for the Vietnamese market's potential, on an absolute and relative basis, Vietnam has one of the smallest venture capital (VC) markets in Asia. While financialisation has accompanied, or even propelled, the East Asian success stories (see the Introduction to this Special Issue), equity financing for fast growing, high-technology small and medium-sized enterprises (SMEs) is underdeveloped in Vietnam (OECD, 2011, p. 7). Fast-paced economic growth, inward FDI flows, and growing technology industries, such as Vietnam's, typically coincide with dynamic VC markets. China, as an example, has seen exponential growth in its VC market since 2000, with the country raising USD 10 billion in VC money in the first half of 2011 alone (AVCJ, 2011). In light of its phenomenal economic growth and the development of its technology sector, it is worth asking why the constitution of a VC market in Vietnam has lagged behind its peers. The slow growth of the VC market is often explained as resulting from the state's historic control of the banking industry, restrictions on foreign investment, regulations limiting the industries in which private companies can compete, insufficient private company reporting requirements and the lack of a regulatory VC framework (Groh et al., 2011). Until the establishment of Vietnam's first stock exchange in 2000, the lack of initial public offering (IPO) exit opportunities was also blamed for Vietnam's undersized VC market (Sack and McKenzie, 1998; Zavatta, 2008). Another explanation is that the Vietnamese government has not incentivised VC market activity as some of its Southeast Asian peers have. As a result, the few VCs operating in Vietnam lament that the fledgling market has grown "despite the regulatory environment, not because of it" (Author interview, Hong Kong, 20 December 2011).

Given Vietnam's Socialist market orientation, level of development and foreign MNC dominance of the technology sector, the country's lack of government policy for

VC may not be altogether puzzling. As one would have expected, Vietnamese policymakers never emphasised VC markets during the 1990s, but during the last decade the CPV has expressed an interest in supporting SME financing. In fact, in 2006 the Ministry of Science and Technology (MoST) even announced plans for a USD 28 million Venture Capital Fund (VCF) that would disburse loans to Vietnamese high-technology SMEs (Intellasia, 2006; Zavatta, 2008). Such SME financing discussions first appeared in Vietnam's public policy language in 2003 as Prime Minister Decision 51 prioritised the promotion of generic domestic capital markets to support Vietnam's growing ICT industry. In this vein, the World Bank-organised multi-actor Consultative Group (CG)'s 2010 mid-year meeting concluded that a more developed capital market was needed for Vietnam's continued technology sector growth (Ministry of Finance, 2010). Policy efforts to enhance the capital available for SMEs further materialised as the Ministry for Planning and Investment (MPI)'s Agency for SME Development (ASMED) received approval for a SME Development Fund in April 2013. The SME Development Fund has a primarily ODA-funded budget of 2 trillion đồng (equivalent to approximately USD 96 million) via Prime Minister Decision 601/QĐ-TTg, 2013 (Talk Vietnam, 2012; Author email exchange with ASMED manager, 20 May 2013). Also, Vietnam's 2011–15 Five Year Plan for SME Development's priority is financing. Yet, to date the CPV has only implemented initiatives that support the provision of credit (not equity) financing to SMEs.

This article asks why VC policies have been slow to materialise, and why they have focused on direct SME loans rather than equity financing over the last decade. I argue that Vietnam's late, credit-based VC policy efforts are the result of both external and domestic factors: ODA donors have not recommended Western-style VC to Vietnamese policymakers, Vietnamese policymakers' incentive structures favour credit financing solutions, policymaking abilities for complex policy areas are poorly resourced, and interest groups (especially the VC market participants) have not sought government attention. Of their own volition, Vietnam's policymakers have requested help from the donor community on SME financing due to that sector's insufficient access to early-stage financing, burgeoning tech SMEs, desire to diversify away from its equitising SOEs (Nguyen et al., 2009), competition for capital, and its policymakers' interest in replicating the East Asian high-technology development successes. In response, donors are not suggesting equity-focused VC policy efforts, although their private sector partner organisations (such as the World Bank's International Finance Corporation – IFC – and infoDev) are providing equity-based solutions to private sector actors. The confluence of these international and domestic forces has resulted in Vietnamese ministers pursuing credit-based SME financing policies rather than equity-based VC policies at a time when their Southeast Asian peers have embraced orthodox VC policies.

This article proceeds as follows. The first section defines VC and gives a brief overview of the Vietnamese VC market today. The second section introduces a policy diffusion framework that helps to identify the mechanisms by which VC policies have been shaped in Vietnam. The third and fourth sections (respectively) detail the international factors and domestic context, including the policymaking process, norms, interest groups and economic conditions, that have impacted Vietnam's VC policymaking. The article draws upon extensive primary material gathered from interviews with Vietnamese policymakers, donors and VC managers in Hanoi, Ho Chi Minh City, Hong Kong and Singapore between December 2011 and September 2012. It has also made extensive use of secondary material – including local news sources, government reports and communiqués and academic literature. The article concludes with an assessment of both international and domestic factors to determine which have had priority and a discussion of what this investigation can tell us about the drivers of financialisation strategies in Asia's late developers.

Venture Capital in Vietnam

Venture Capital (VC) is defined here as financial capital provided to SMEs with high growth potential in exchange for company equity.[1] VC is a subset of the alternative investment class of private equity (PE), which refers to investments in companies that are "unlisted" or not publicly traded. VC is high-risk and illiquid, with VC managers investing in start-ups for their potential to yield exceptional investment returns. In a portfolio of ten companies, for example, VC managers might expect just one company to be an outstanding performer, with others expected to fail or muddle along. In the United States, the VC market gained notoriety by investing in huge growth companies (e.g. Google and Facebook). By the late 1990s, the global VC market managed over USD 100 billion (Gompers and Lerner, 1999). Despite its growth, the VC industry is still relatively small in terms of assets under management (AuM); at the end of 2012 the global hedge fund industry had nearly USD 2 trillion AuM (BarclayHedge, 2012) and sovereign wealth funds (SWFs) managed more than USD 5 trillion (SWF Institute, 2012). While the size of VC assets managed is small in comparison, VC is said to have a big impact on national economies. The National VC Association (NVCA) in the US, for example, found that while the VC market accounted for only 0.2 per cent of American GDP, 21 per cent of companies (in GDP terms) have been backed by VC funds (NVCA, 2011).

Notably, VC has become an increasingly international market, with governments devising public policies in the expectation of creating a local "Silicon Valley". Public policies for supporting VC include three primary elements. The first is government funding, with states either investing in privately managed VC funds or providing initial investment to VC managers via a funds of VC funds (FoVCF) structure. A FoVCF is a pool of capital invested into VC funds, rather than a fund that invests directly in start-ups. Tax treatment comprises the second element of public policy deemed crucial in the formation of VC. Here, tax policy includes the way in which VC profits are categorised for tax purposes – either as capital gains, income, corporate or tax exempt – as well as incentives on offer for investors (e.g. tax credits). The third element of VC policy relates to legal and regulatory frameworks, including regulations on foreign investor participation and the adoption of VC structures such as the Anglo-American limited partnership (LP) or the Japanese company structure. Importantly, states have utilised a combination of these VC policy instruments (funding, taxation and regulation) to build and oversee private VC markets.

To this end, today nearly 90 per cent of the OECD, Group of 20 (G-20) and Asian Tiger countries have launched public initiatives aimed at growing equity-based VC market activity (Klingler-Vidra, 2014). This international spread of VC policies began in the late 1970s, when governments and international organisations (IOs) began identifying an insufficient amount of investment capital available for high-technology SMEs as a roadblock to building their local Silicon Valley. Filling the "equity gap" for early-stage companies has also been identified as enhancing economic activity and innovation (OECD, 1996). IOs, particularly the OECD and the World Bank, have promulgated VC policy advice (see OECD, 2003). In addition, states have learned from and emulated each other's VC policies. For example, Singaporean policymakers, recognising the success of the US Silicon Valley, "placed particular emphasis on the development of a venture capital industry in Singapore to boost the development of technology start-ups and entrepreneurship" (Bruton et al., 2002, p. 199).

Among Vietnam's Southeast Asian peers, Malaysia was an early standout in VC with nearly USD 1 billion in VC AuM by 2003 (AVCJ, 2005). Part of Malaysia's success in developing its equity-based VC market is attributed to policies that established a regulatory framework and provided public funding for the asset class. For example, the Malaysia Venture Capital Management Berhad (MAVCAP), a government FoVCF, was established in 2001 by the Ministry of Finance to support both the Malaysian ICT sector and the domestic VC industry (Malaysia Venture Capital Management Berhad, 2012). Indonesia, though a slow starter in VC fundraising, has recently received significant attention as "the next China" in light of its demographic and economic trends (AVCJ, 2011, p. 5). VC managers' excitement about Indonesian VC investment comes after the Indonesian government began supporting VC domestically in 1988. The first VC policy initiative in Indonesia was Presidential Decree No. 61, which defined what a VC firm is and how it is overseen (Business Review, 2010). More recently, the Minister of Finance issued Regulation No. 18/PMK.010/2012 regarding Venture Capital Companies (ABNR Law, 2012). Thus, Southeast Asian states have supported VC markets via combinations of the three globally orthodox VC policy elements. Figures 1 and 2 illustrate the flow of VC money into Southeast Asian funds. In doing so, they highlight the modest amount of VC activity in the high-growth Vietnamese economy.

The VC industry in Vietnam remains underdeveloped, although green shoots of a Vietnamese VC market were concurrent with economic liberalisation in the 1990s. At the onset of the Asian financial crisis, most of the eight VC firms in Vietnam, which managed approximately USD 400 million and were all foreign, left the market (Zavatta, 2008). A new batch of VC firms started to operate in the early 2000s, yet the number of players and investments has remained modest. Vietnam's small VC market has

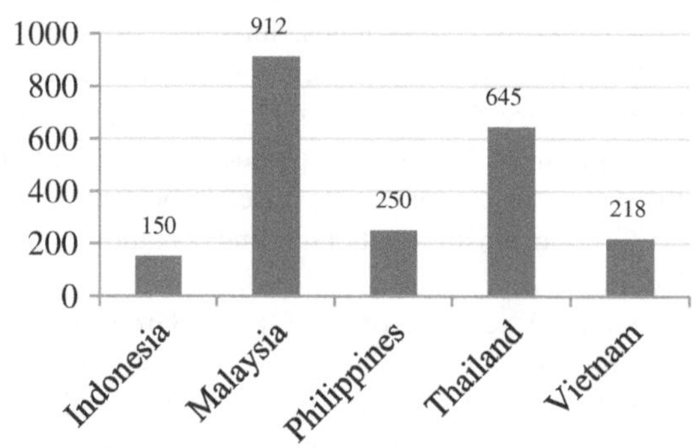

Figure 1. VC Market AuM (in USD million)

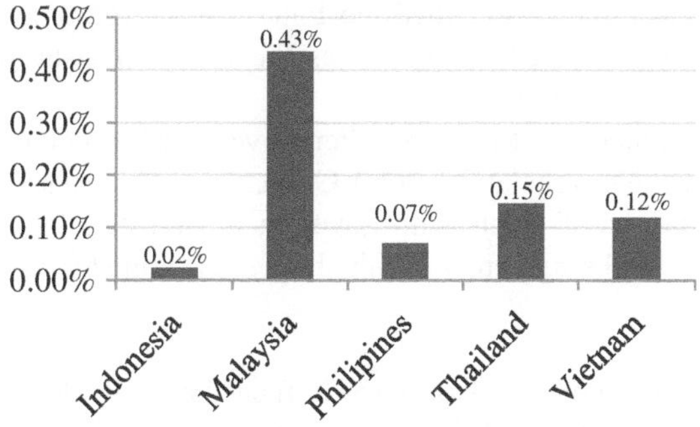

Figure 2. VC market AuM (as per cent of GDP)
Source: AVCJ (2005); Note for Figure 2: In 2003 GDP for each country was as follows: Indonesia's USD 666 billion, Malaysia's USD 210 billion, Philippines' USD 356 billion, Thailand's USD 429 billion, Vietnam's USD 183 billion. GDP figures were used to calculate VC as a percent of national GDP for each country.

oscillated between peak AuM of USD 318 million in 1999 and just over USD 150 million (AVCJ, 2005; AltAssets, 2011). At present, there are four PE/VC firms operating in Vietnam with approximately USD 150 million under management; they are IDG Ventures Vietnam, DFJ VinaVentures, Dragon Capital, and Mekong Capital (AltAssets, 2011; Chen, 2010).

National funds to support the technology sector and SME financing have been initiated by the MoST (the 2006 VCF), the Science, Technology and Environment Committee via their 2007 discussion of a USD 30 million fund for high-technology SMEs (Zavatta, 2008), and the MPI (the 2013 SME Development Fund). These funds have been designed for SMEs directly in the form of loans, not equity investments. According to Prime Minister Decision 601/QĐ-TTg (dated 17 April 2013), the SME Development Fund offers "preferential interest rate loans at an interest rate 90% cheaper than financial markets" rather than equity investments in SMEs (Author email exchange with ASMED manager, 20 May 2013). Similarly, in Resolution No. 22/NQ-CP on 5 May 2010, which details the plans for implementing Government Decree No. 56/2009/ ND-CP on supporting the development of SMEs, there was no mention of "venture capital" or "equity". Instead, an entire section (II) of the Resolution is dedicated to the "accessibility of credit capital sources". The resolution dictates the following actions for the MPI in implementing SME financing support

> negotiating, receiving or arranging official development assistance (ODA) sources to provide technical assistance and enhance capabilities for credit institutions to expand their credit to small-or-medium-sized enterprises … and submitting to the Prime Minister a report on the application of credit mechanisms and policies … and proposing measures to boost the development of products and services suitable to small- and medium-sized enterprises, such as factoring and financing leasing (Socialist Republic of Vietnam, 2010).

The SME Development Fund (also called the Enterprise Development Fund) carries on the tradition of focusing on credit solutions as the Fund consists of low interest rate loans rather than equity investments.

Vietnam has not adopted the LP, or an alternative, legal structure explicitly for VC fund managers. Rather than regulations for VC managers, licences for VC managers to operate have come via one-off deals with government ministers, as in the case of IDG Ventures Vietnam. In IDG's agreement with the MoST minister in exchange for their licence they agreed to

> help to market and promote the Hoa Lac Hi-Tech Park outside Vietnam and provide advice and support to the Ministry as it plans construction and operation of a High-Tech Conference and Exposition Centre in Hoa Lac Hi-Tech Park (IDG Ventures Vietnam, 2007).

The IDG agreement exemplifies the individual, inconsistent nature of policymakers' involvement with the VC market, rather than their transparent offering of VC industry-wide incentives or access. Limitations on foreign ownership of local companies and capital controls remain, despite 2007 WTO accession, impeding VC managers' ability to buy and sell shares in Vietnamese start-ups (Freeman and Le, 2007; Do, 2008; Freeman, 2004). In addition, VC profits continue to be taxed at the general corporate tax rate of 25 per cent – although the VC managers operating in Vietnam are domiciled offshore so the Vietnamese tax rate does not affect them. In sum, VC has entered into the awareness of policymakers in Vietnam, particularly those responsible for SME support policies, but VC policy measures remain demonstrably elusive – especially those akin to the global trend of offering regulatory, tax and funding policies to support early-stage equity financing.

A Policy Diffusion Framework for Understanding VC Policies in Vietnam

In this section a policy diffusion framework is employed to detail the international and domestic drivers contributing to the nature of VC policy in Vietnam. Policy diffusion analytical tools have been deployed in international political economy (IPE) circles, as scholars looked at the relationship between increased capital mobility and the attempts by states to attract and retain capital. Findings, such as those presented by Simmons and Elkins (2004), speak to the constraining impact that the diffusion of policy ideas had on policymakers, resulting in a convergence towards neoliberal market policies. Over time, policy diffusion, institutional isomorphism (DiMaggio and Powell, 1983) and policy transfer (Dolowitz and Marsh, 2000) research has expanded beyond focusing upon economic competition and learning mechanisms. Now, policy diffusion includes realist (coercion) and liberal (competition), as well as rationalist (learning) and constructivist (emulation) strands, contributing to identifying the primary drivers behind policy outcomes. Policy diffusion research has tended to prioritise the investigation of which states are looked to (whether geographically proximate, culturally similar, etc), instead of assessing the impact of the domestic context on policy diffusion (Lenschow et al., 2005). Scholars have, however, called for greater "inside-out" investigation of domestic factors on diffusion, or transmutation, outcomes (see Painter, 2005; Yeo and Painter, 2011). This line of research has also uncovered how the multiplicity of source models (see Falkner and Gupta, 2009) or the domestic context (see Weyland, 2006; Yeo and Painter, 2011) may lead to divergent, rather than convergent, policy outcomes. In an extension of the work of these authors, this article employs a policy diffusion framework that *gives equal priority to domestic and international factors* in its investigation of the sources of Vietnam's unique VC policy approach.

The analytical framework of policy diffusion used by Simmons, Dobbin and Garrett (2008) harnesses the S-shaped curve of innovation (Rogers, 1995) to explain why, how and when policies are diffused. The framework offers all four policy diffusion mechanisms listed above, encompassing rationalist and constructivist ontologies: coercion, competition, learning and emulation. On the one hand, the learning and emulation mechanisms are the more proactive variety, as they involve, in different ways, a state choosing to replicate a policy utilised elsewhere. On the other hand, economic competition and coercion are more reactive in nature. Policymakers are pushed to deploy policies because it is necessary from a competitive perspective, or as the result of a relatively more powerful actor (either state or IO) forcing policy change.

Learning and emulation involve domestic policymakers seeking external policy options and evidence. Learning occurs when policymakers evaluate and then choose elements of policies that have been successfully deployed elsewhere (Berry and Baybeck, 2005; Busch and Jorgens, 2005). Learning also occurs as policymakers design policies for new issue areas with which they are not familiar. Whereas policy learning has the policymakers focused on evidence, policy emulation is a mechanism in which policymakers imitate other government policies in an effort to appear similar (Shipan and Volden, 2008). Imitation is juxtaposed to policy learning in which policymakers are interested in understanding the precise design, deployment and measurement of policies. Emulation implies that policymakers worked to appear to be similar to other states, either "the leader" (e.g. the US in the global VC market) or "successful peers" (e.g. East Asian states), without engaging in in-depth research. To ascertain whether learning or the "me too" emulation mechanism is at work, researchers examine the extent to which policymakers researched alternative policies and had evidence of policy outcomes before employing local prescriptions.

Economic competition and coercion, while quite different from one another, are characterised by their shared focus on external forces shaping domestic policy choice sets. Power asymmetries are essential to coercion, just as the need for international capital is essential to competition. Economic competition may occur when states compete to attract and retain capital, whether FDI or portfolio investments. As Simmons and Elkins (2004) argued, the adoption of policies in competing states changes the competitive landscape. Economic competition has been investigated by determining the policymakers' concern that capital would be redirected elsewhere (e.g. Berry and Baybeck, 2005). Coercion is characterised by conditions being placed on policymakers by outside actors. Coercion may involve a relatively more powerful state implementing trade sanctions against another state to force the adoption of its desired policy. Coercion could also occur when an IO requires economic reforms as a condition for funding or membership.

At the crux of this article's investigation is whether Vietnam's current heterodox VC policy form is the result of domestic or exogenous forces. The external evidence is expected to come from the IOs and other states coercing VC policy prescriptions on Vietnam, either through IO funding conditionality, IO membership rules, or international competitive pressures. On the domestic front, the article examines the impact of economic management norms and Vietnam's economic structure on VC policymaking. In reality, the external and internal are more interrelated than presented here, as the two arenas may shape each other. Despite this oversimplification, the analytical delineation enables an examination of the external and internal sources of Vietnam's heterodox VC policy outcome.

International Factors

Have international actors and pressures shaped the credit-focused nature of VC policies in Vietnam? Vietnam's vibrant donor community, which includes more than 50 IOs and states, has promulgated capital market development advice to the Vietnamese government (see World Bank, 2012). This advice carries weight in Vietnam, as the Socialist Republic continues to be one of the world's largest recipients of ODA (Thoburn, 2009), with one third of the CPV's public budget coming from ODA (Aid Effectiveness, 2012). In addition, trade agreements since the 1990s have established Vietnam's economic links, notably ASEAN and the Framework Agreement on Economic Cooperation with the European Union in 1995, APEC in 1998, the US bilateral trade agreement in 2000 and WTO accession in 2007. Vietnam has been increasingly competing in the global economy ever since.

In tandem with these interactions, reports and advice on SME financing and capital market development have come from several donors and trade partners. The external actors who have been most active in advising CPV ministers on SME financing have been the Japanese, the World Bank, the UN, the ADB and APEC (Author interview, Hanoi, 21 August 2012). The World Bank-led CG forum helped to introduce SME financing to the MPI's policy agenda in the early 2000s but has not suggested equity-financing policies. The UN, in a 2007 report on SME financing in Vietnam, recommended that the state not intervene:

> this report proposes that there is relatively little that ASMED can (or should) usefully do, at least in a direct fashion, to improve SMEs' access to finance (Freeman and Le, 2007, p. 7).

Sentiment about the applicability of VC policy to Vietnam, as expressed by the Director of the SME working group of a regional IO, was that the Socialist Republic is "not developed enough for sophisticated capital markets such as VC" (Author interview, Singapore, 24 September 2012). Rather than advise CPV policymakers directly, a recent APEC report commented that "as Vietnam is a late-comer, it needs to thoroughly analyse the policies applied by other countries in order to be able to compete with them in attracting venture capital" (Chen, 2010). Thus, donor assessments have suggested that Vietnamese policymakers refrain from enacting equity-based policy to improve the SME financing environment or from conducting research themselves. Instead, donors have continued to allocate loans to Vietnamese SMEs via government hands. As a result, even the ODA-funded SME Development Fund deliberations focused on "low interest rate loans directly to SMEs", rather than on equity-based allocations to VCs or start-ups (Author interview, Hanoi, 21 August 2012).

The IOs' private sector development partnerships in Vietnam, on the other hand, have provided equity investments and equity financing policy advice. In this way, the only equity-financing efforts in Vietnam have come in the form of donors' partners working "around the state" (Carroll, 2012) rather than through it. As an example, the World Bank Group's IFC was a seed investor for the Ho Chi Minh City-based VC manager Mekong Capital at its launch in 2001 (Author interview, Ho Chi Minh City, 22 August 2012). The IFC's Mekong Private Sector Development Facility invested in Mekong's VC fund as it aimed to create sustainable, for-profit businesses in Vietnam. In addition, in 2008 InfoDev published a report on the opportunities and challenges associated with financing high-tech SMEs in Vietnam. The report suggested that greater support for equity financing would be beneficial for the market (Zavatta, 2008). More recently, InfoDev has funded private SME accelerators, including the Start Network and TOPICA in Ho Chi Minh City (Author interview, Ho Chi Minh City, 23 August 2012). So, while loan-based methods continue to be designed for the state, innovative equity-financing efforts have been directed to Vietnam's private sector actors.

It was hoped that Vietnam's 2007 WTO accession would improve the environment for VC investment, but to date it has had a limited impact. Technology, a favourite industry for VC investors, was named in the Socialist Republic's WTO Schedule of Specific Commitments in Services as a sector where foreigners can buy up to 100 per cent of company equity (WTO, 2006). Vietnam's domestic regulations (e.g. Decree 139/2007/ND-CP) have nevertheless continued to refine what is included in these commitments such that foreign investors' access to ownership in unlisted Vietnamese companies remains limited, even in "committed" sectors (Tran, 2012). Interviews with Vietnamese entrepreneurs and VC managers similarly echoed that the broad implementation of WTO commitments is still lacking due to government decrees (Author interviews, Ho Chi Minh City, 22, 23 and 24 August 2012). Issues identified in a 2007 UNIDO report on SME financing in Vietnam similarly included VC funds' inability to invest in more than 30 per cent of an unlisted private company's equity (and 49 per cent of a public company's ownership) (Freeman and Le, 2007). Managers at three of the four VC firms operating in Vietnam lamented that the environment for investing in Vietnamese companies has not become transparent or predictable as a result of the 2007 WTO accession. With that said, VC managers expect that the 2014 phase of adherence to commitments will open foreign investment beyond the 30 per cent equity cap across more sectors (Author interviews, Ho Chi Minh City, 22 and 23 August 2012). It is hoped that future investors' access will not be subject to the provincial Departments of Planning and Investment (DPIs') differing interpretations of Decrees and WTO commitments when the new phase begins (Canadian Trade Commissioner, 2011). Taken together, we find that WTO rules have not coerced sweeping regulatory changes for VC investments in Vietnam.

Private foreign actors have played a role in bringing VC into the Socialist Republic, as Vietnam's VC managers are either foreigners or returning expats. In the late 1990s it was returning Vietnamese who had studied in the United States, as well as foreigners, who introduced the VC asset class to Vietnam. Of the four VC managers operating in Vietnam today, at least half spent a significant amount of time working and studying in the United States, and founders of two of the firms are foreign. IDG Ventures' Managing Director is Henry Nguyen, who spent significant time in the United States. Henry was an Associate at Goldman Sachs in New York, completed his BA at Harvard

University and earned his MD and MBA from Northwestern University. Mekong Capital's founder and Managing Director, Chris Freund, is an American with significant experience in Asia, and nearly 20 years of investment experience in Vietnam. The Managing Director of DFJ VinaCapital Partners' VC investment portfolio is Than Trong Phuc, who worked at Intel for 23 years. Phuc joined Intel in Santa Clara, CA, in 1986 and relocated to Vietnam by leading Intel Vietnam beginning in 1999. In addition, Dragon Capital's senior management team is composed of two types: foreigners with significant investment experience in emerging Asia, and Vietnamese with academic, and professional, experience in Europe or the United States.

Finally, CPV policymakers have taken capital market policy inspiration, as well as advice, from other states. Vietnam has studied its "economically successful Asian neighbours" given the CPV's coupling of capitalist economic management with single-party leadership (Turley and Selden, 1993, pp. 3–4). In this vein, the Vietnamese Foreign Ministry and diplomatic missions "collect economic and technical information" and share it with national economic ministries and regional authorities (Vu, 2003, p. 48). As an example, Prime Minister's Decision No. 151 established the State Capital Investment Corporation (SCIC) to manage the capital from SOE equitisations in 2005, naming Singapore's Temasek Holdings as the model (World Bank, 2006, p. 20). In addition, the Japanese *keiretsu* – the term given to Japanese companies with shared ownership and related business lines – helped inspire Vietnamese SOEs' conglomerate structures in the 1990s (Perkins and Vu, 2009, p. 32). In fact, Japan was identified as the country most central to Vietnamese SME policymakers' learning from abroad as Japan most proactively sends "experts to provide technical assistance to the ASMED team" (Author interview, Hanoi, 21 August 2012). Japan, even more than other Asian states that use loans rather than only equity instruments as VC, was slow to adopt an internationally compatible VC regulatory structure and government funding (Kenney et al., 2002). Japanese advice on SME support in Vietnam has been focused on credit-based solutions, akin to its VC market at home.

Domestic Factors

Domestic factors have had enabling and constraining impacts on VC market-building policy efforts. In Vietnam, as in some of its Asian neighbours, the state has controlled a deliberate market transition. Starting with the *doi moi* (renovation) reforms in 1986, and followed by a new Constitution in the 1990s and Enterprise Laws in the 2000s, the Vietnamese market has inched forward in its Socialist market economy transition (Forsberg and Kokko, 2007, p. 1; JICA, 2003, p. 4). Beginning with *doi moi*, but then increasingly in the new millennium, the state's role has slowly shifted from that of a financier with central authority over credit allocation decisions via the state-owned banks (Perkins and Vu, 2009) to that of a market facilitator that empowers FDI through the creation of initiatives such as enterprise zones, industrial zones and export processing zones (Painter, 2005; Thoburn, 2009). Even the *doi moi* reforms are said to have been driven not by the collapse of the Soviet Union or a great ideological shift, but instead by the government's response to a severe domestic economic recession (Phan, 2003, p. 24) and the playing out of rival state-business interests (Gainsborough, 2002). Neoliberal policies have not been uniformly understood to be a retreat of the Vietnamese state, but instead a new form of the state's interventionism that allows the state to extract value from firms such as its equitised SOEs (Gainsborough, 2009). Thus, Vietnamese policymakers, though "dependent on capital inflows to feed growth" are "not a mendicant" before their donors (Painter, 2005, p. 277). In sum, Vietnamese policymakers contend that their march towards neoliberal economic management has been done at the behest of the CPV and not the cajoling of the IMF[2] or World Bank. So, Vietnamese policymakers have agency over policy outcomes. But what drives their policy decisions?

Domestic economic forces have increased the relevance of VC policies to Vietnamese policymakers. The ICT industry has recently taken off in Vietnam, as evidenced by the massive facility investments by ICT MNCs and growing tech SME activity. Beginning in around 2004, Vietnam emerged with mobile gaming and search start-ups that have drawn investment from foreign MNCs and VCs for their cloning of successful business models elsewhere for the Vietnamese market (Fannin, 2011, p. 13). Given the dependence of VC markets on the existence of technology entrepreneurship, VC markets have become relevant to Vietnam as the domestic technology capacity has advanced in the last decade. Thus, a functionalist argument could be made that VC markets were not relevant to Vietnam before the twenty-first century. The pragmatic CPV policymakers only started discussing VC policy as they became aware of VC's relevance to the Socialist Republic. Although the late development of ICT entrepreneurship in Vietnam can explain the late timing of VC policy interest, it does not explain the credit form of Vietnam's nascent VC policies.

Vietnam's existing VC managers have not sought out government support for their industry; instead, they prefer to stay "off the radar" of the CPV and away from unruly "red tape" (Author interviews, Ho Chi Minh City, 22 and 24 August 2012). The sentiment that government involvement is to be avoided rather than sought out is consistent with other scholars' empirical findings that operating within reach of the Vietnamese state was "frequently predatory" (Gainsborough, 2009, p. 268). VC managers interviewed in Ho Chi Minh City did not believe that they would benefit from government involvement in their industry, and instead felt that the "informal advantages" they had from operating in a non-transparent market could be substantial. Moreover, they expressed sentiment that (corrupt) state actors would only become involved when they wanted to extract payments. This article would be remiss if it did not mention that one of the VC managers, Henry Nguyen of IDG Ventures, is the son-in-law of Prime Minister Nguyen Tan Dung (Fannin, 2011, p. 67). Mr Nguyen, despite his academic accolades in the United States and his technical background, may represent the type of private sector actor able to succeed in Vietnam as a result of close personal relations with state officials. Sentiment among private participants in the Vietnamese market and academics alike is that such effective "sponsorships" from well-placed CPV members are essential to their "competitive advantage" (Author interviews, Ho Chi Minh City, 23 and 24 August 2012; Painter, 2005, p. 269). The example of the high-growth company VNG (formerly VinaGame) was given in several interviews as a successful business that lost its government sponsor or became too successful for the government to not want to partake in its profits.[3] Sentiment was that VNG's public listing was precluded by government enquiries into its business (Author interviews, Ho Chi Minh City, 22, 23 and 24 August 2012).

The credit-centric nature of the Vietnamese financial sector and the importance of securing ODA loans have contributed to the state's reluctance about equity-based financing. Vietnam's finance sector is overwhelmingly bank, not capital market, based. In fact, financial services in Vietnam were wholly run by five state-owned banks through 2000 when the state started liberalising the banking sector. The banks had complete control over the allocation of credit – which largely went to SOEs – thus depriving private companies of access to financing to grow their businesses. Notably, there has been acknowledgment that bank-provided credit is not sufficient for growing SMEs. The official WTO accession report stated that "only 32.4 per cent of SMEs have qualified for formal bank loans", so alternative financing had to be sought for them to be competitive (Ministry of Industry and Trade, 2007, p. 220). Although ASMED policymakers demonstrated their awareness of the need for alternative financing forms, including VC markets, they did not consider equity-based investments for the SME Development Fund (Author interviews, Hanoi, 21 August 2012; Author email exchange, 20 May 2013). Instead, these policymakers, in line with Resolution 56, demonstrated their preference for securing ODA-funded credit-based financing solutions. As the MPI is centrally responsible for managing relationships with Vietnam's donors, their securing of large funding initiatives, such as through the SME Development Fund, helps them to "demonstrate success" (Author interview, Hanoi, 21 August 2012). The securing of further ODA money, rather than considering the products and services that may best serve Vietnam's next stage of development, is domestic policymakers' priority. As a result, policymakers have not sought out possible equity-based solutions for developing Vietnam's technopreneurship. The bank instead of capital market (e.g. credit instead of equity) orientation in Vietnam is consistent with the situation in other East Asian states (Whitley, 1992). However, even in highly bank-centric economies, such as Hong Kong and Singapore, the state adopted VC policies in the 1990s. In credit-based Japan it took the state until the new millennium to improve the regulatory environment for equity investors in an effort to aid SME growth and innovation via equity investments.

Related to the bank-centric character of the economy, Vietnamese policymakers, as well as entrepreneurs, are driven by the norm that bank loans are the primary way to raise money. As an illustration of the mistrust of equity financing, an early-stage equity investor shared a story of a Vietnamese entrepreneur who took the cheque he received from an equity investor and bought a brand new USD 200,000 BMW (Author interview, Ho Chi Minh City, 24 August 2012). An equity investment, as understood by the entrepreneur, was "money for nothing" since he did not have to make payments on a loan and had no collateral that could be called upon. A similar sentiment was expressed in another interview, in which a successful Vietnamese entrepreneur was described as someone who had "raised money from an investor, rather than an entrepreneur who successfully exited via an IPO or trade sale" (Author interview, Ho Chi Minh City, 23 August 2012). The persistence of a predisposition towards credit-lending, and the newness of the concept of equity-based financing in Vietnam, have meant that domestic policymakers do not yet think in terms of equity policy solutions.

Vietnam's "decentralised, fragmented and sometimes incoherent" (Painter, 2005, p. 267) domestic policymaking institutions also help to explain the slow deployment of the initial VC policy efforts. Vietnam's policymakers struggle to convert ideas for complex policy areas into implemented policies (Ohno, 2009). This is due to ministerial coordination, capacity and information problems (see OECD, 2011, p.10; Vu, 2003). Scholars such as Martin Gainsborough have found that policy implementation in SOE equitisation has been "slow and incremental" (2002, p. 390). The VC industry's oversight exemplifies the decentralised and uncoordinated nature of Vietnamese policy-making that contributes to these slow policy outcomes. The VC market is overseen at the national level by the MoST. However, funding and policy coordination for SMEs, including SME financing, is managed by the MPI's ASMED and the budget comes from the State Bank and the Ministry of Finance (Author interview, Hanoi, 20 August 2012). The complex and uncoordinated nature of policymaking helps to explain why the SME Development Fund only received approval in April 2013, even though the ASMED team had prepared the draft for the Prime Minister's Office review in 2011.

The extent to which Vietnamese policymakers have been able to study equity-based VC policy options is also questionable. ASMED managers described "Google Scholar" as "a key source of information", and said that their research benefited from the proactive information brought to them from Japanese experts and the semi-annual APEC SME working group meetings (Author interviews, Hanoi, 21 August 2012). Although the APEC forum was mentioned as a critical resource, the extent to which the Vietnamese ASMED delegates actively engaged in the APEC meetings was questioned in subsequent interviews with other participants in the SME workshops. Participants described the Vietnamese representatives' involvement as "limited and passive", given their "inability to communicate effectively" (Author interview, Singapore, 24 September 2012). Given the limited resources of the ASMED team and its reliance on Japanese expertise, we begin to understand why equity-based VC policy information has not been sought out by Vietnamese policymakers.

Conclusion

Vietnamese policymakers are not merely at the mercy of their donors' priorities. Long before external forces pushed Vietnamese policymakers towards a neoliberal transition, Vietnam initiated institutional reforms and liberalisation programs, beginning with *doi moi* reforms in 1986. The CPV's ability to push back on donors stems from their exceptional economic success since market opening in the late 1980s. Donors have been found to accept adapted implementations of their initiatives (as well as institutionalised corruption) due to their desire to remain associated with the Vietnamese development success story (Carroll, 2012). But, in the VC policy area, what should we make of the relative weights of the external and domestic sources of Vietnam's credit-based SME financing policies to date? Has Vietnam been coerced into or away from equity-based VC policy? Or, has the credit preference of Vietnamese policymakers steered ODA towards loans for SMEs?

International donors have had an impact on Vietnamese SME policymakers' agenda setting and policy choices through their funding and technical assistance. By and large, although Vietnam's donor community has discussed VC, it has not recommended, let alone pushed, equity-focused VC policies for Vietnam. WTO membership rules have not forced open investment access for the foreign-domiciled VC funds operating in Vietnam or encouraged VC-specific policies. Nor have donors, through their policy advice (e.g. the UNIDO report) and forums (e.g. the World Bank CG), encouraged the state to deploy equity-based financing for SMEs. Donors have recommended that Vietnam learn from other states, particularly East Asian success stories, to build its technology sector and capital markets, but they have not instructed Vietnamese policymakers to replicate the VC models. Instead, the IOs' support of VC markets has gone around the state, as the private sector development partners (the IFC and InfoDev) have made equity investments directly in private VCs and SME accelerators. External private actors, particularly returning Vietnamese, have also brought in knowledge of VC markets. They have preferred to operate in the opaque regulatory environment as it offers a competitive advantage. The result is that private actors possess knowledge about the VC industry, but policies for an equity-based VC industry have not been pushed on the Socialist Republic's policymakers.

To this end, Vietnamese policymakers continue to create policies focused on loans, as they are not compelled by domestic pressures to act in the VC industry arena. Moreover, prevailing norms favour credit-based solutions, incentivising the maximising of ODA funding and dovetailing with limited institutional capacity to proactively learn about such complex, niche capital markets. Domestic policymakers have elicited SME financing advice from donors, but financial and technical assistance has focused on credit-based solutions rather than equity investments. Vietnamese SME policymakers have not sent missions to other states to learn about their VC policy experiences and have instead harnessed "desktop research" focused on tools such as Google Scholar. The limited expertise as a result of the poor environment for policy learning has reinforced MPI policymakers' reliance on donors to help them formulate SME financing policies. The poorly resourced departments responsible for SME financing policies face problems similar to scholarly findings about poor public administration reform more broadly (see Acuña-Alfaro, 2009).

Both external and domestic factors have played a role in directing Vietnamese policymakers away from traditional equity-based VC policies in favour of credit financing solutions. As a result, although VC markets have been introduced into policymakers' agendas, policy efforts aimed at improving equity-based SME financing have not yet materialised and Vietnam's nascent VC policies are diverging from the international norm of equity-based solutions. Donors were not found to coerce Vietnam to adopt VC policy recommendations as has been the case with other states, and in fact recommended the avoidance of supply-side, complex policies in some cases. Domestically, the growth of high-technology SME activity and its contribution to the Vietnamese economy has led to the state's interest in SME financing, but has not propelled equity-based policies. Vietnam's normative bias towards credit-based schemes, limited policymaking capacity (especially in complex arenas), and donors' continued promotion of the use of loans for SME financial support have combined to shape the credit-financing nature of VC policies in Vietnam.

The diffusion of VC policies has been happening globally, including across the Southeast Asian states of Malaysia, Indonesia and Thailand. Late developers, such as Vietnam and its Southeast Asian peers, are examining these various paths and adapting the strategies to their domestic contexts. To this end, Malaysia and Indonesia have embraced VC market policies through government FoVCFs and VC-specific regulations, but such equity-based VC policy steps have not materialised in Vietnam. It is implied by the analysis in this article that unless there is a normative shift among Vietnamese policymakers and their ODA consultants in favour of supporting equity-based financing, or until Vietnamese policymakers are better able to independently learn about and implement policies for complex capital markets, the diffusion of VC ideas will continue to translate into a divergent, credit-based outcome in Hanoi.

Notes

1. VC, as a subset of private equity, refers to a capital investment in exchange for company equity, but debt instruments can also be used as the collateral for the capital. In Western markets, particularly in the US, investment in exchange for interest-bearing loans is known as "venture lending" rather than VC. But, in some Asian markets, especially Japan, VC is also structured as credit-based investment transactions.
2. The IMF discontinued its financing programs to Vietnam as conditionality regarding transparency into government accounting and spending was not granted in 2004. This lack of transparency was also found by Transparency International in its low ranking of Vietnam (Perkins and Vu, 2009).
3. Vietnam's industrial policymaking process lacks transparency and has institutionalised corruption, which has been noted as a fundamental impediment to further development of Vietnam's economy (see Le, 2010; Gainsborough, 2003).

References

ABNR Law (2012) New regulation on venture capital companies. *ABNR Counsellors at Law News*. Available at http://www.abnrlaw.com/news_detail.php?send_news_id=170&year=2012&month=4, accessed 18 December 2012.

Acuña-Alfaro, Jairo (2009) Reforming public administration in Vietnam: Current situation and recommendations (Hanoi: The National Political Publishing House and the United Nations Development Programme in Vietnam).

Aid Effectiveness (2012) Vietnam country profile. Aid Effectiveness Portal. Available at http://www.aideffectiveness.org/Country-Vietnam.html, accessed 29 October 2012.

AltAssets (2011) Vietnamese private equity industry exits total $150m in 2010. *AltAssets*, 17 January. Available at http://www.altassets.net/private-equity-news/vietnamese-private-equity-industry-exits-total-150m-in-2010.html, accessed 9 October 2012.

AVCJ (Asian Venture Capital Journal) (2005) Asian Private Equity 300 Guide. *AVCJ*.

AVCJ (2011) Asia Pacific Private Equity 2011–2012. *AVCJ*.

BarclayHedge Alternative Investment Databases (2012) Hedge fund industry - Assets under management: 3rd quarter 2012. BarclayHedge. Available at http://www.barclayhedge.com/research/indices/ghs/mum/HF_Money_Under_Management.html, accessed 5 December 2012.

Berry, William D. and Brady Baybeck (2005) Using geographic information systems to study interstate competition. *American Political Science Review* 99(4), pp. 505–19.

Bruton, G.D., D. Ahlstrom and K. Kingh (2002) The impact of the institutional environment on the venture capital industry in Singapore. *Venture Capital: An International Journal of Entrepreneurial Finance* 4(3), pp. 197–218.

Busch, Per-olof and Helge Jörgens (2005) The international sources of policy convergence: Explaining the spread of environmental policy innovations. *Journal of European Public Policy* 12(5), pp. 860–84.

Business Review (2010) Financing institutions other than banks. All About Business Review and Management. Available at http://businessreview-article.blogspot.co.uk/2010/12/financing-institutions-other-than-banks.html, accessed 18 December 2012.

Canadian Trade Commissioner (2011) An investment guide to Vietnam, December. Available at http://www.tradecommissioner.gc.ca/eng/pdf.jsp?did=91398&fn=91398-eng.pdf, accessed 18 December 2012.

Carroll, Toby (2012) Working on, through and around the state: The deep marketisation of development in the Asia-Pacific. *Journal of Contemporary Asia* 42(3), pp. 378–404.

Chen, Ian (2010) Vietnam seeking investment capital from venture funds. APEC Digital Opportunity Center, 1 November. Available at http://www.apecdoc.org/site/vietnam/2010/11/01/vietnam-seeking-investment-capital-from-venture-funds/, accessed 9 October 2012.

DiMaggio, P.J. and W.W. Powell (1983) The iron cage revisited: Institutional isomorphism and collective rationality in organizational fields. *American Sociological Review* 48(2), pp. 147–60.

Do, Khoa D. (2008) Vietnam offers big opportunity for savvy, patient investors. *Venture Capital Journal*, November. Available at http://www.dlapiper.com/files/upload/vcj_nov08.pdf, accessed 9 October 2012.

Dolowitz, D. and D. Marsh (2000) Learning from abroad: The role of policy transfer in contemporary policy-making. *Governance* 13(1), pp. 5–24.

Falkner, Robert and Aarti Gupta (2009) The limits of regulatory convergence: Globalization and GMO politics in the South. *International Environmental Agreements* 9(2), pp. 113–33.

Fannin, Rebecca A. (2011) *Startup Asia: Top strategies for cashing in on Asia's innovation boom* (Singapore: John Wiley and Sons).

Forsberg, Le Thanh and Ari Kokko (2007) The role of donors in Vietnamese development planning. EIJS Working Paper No. 238. Stockholm School of Economics, Stockholm, Sweden. Available at http://swopec.hhs.se/eijswp/papers/eijswp0238.pdf, accessed 9 October 2012.

Freeman, Nick (2004) Expanding horizons: Equity finance in Vietnam. IFC Mekong Private Sector Development Facility Private Sector Discussions No. 16. Available at http://www.ifc.org/ifcext/mekongpsdf.nsf/AttachmentsByTitle/PSDP+16/$FILE/PSDP-No-16-EN.pdf, accessed 9 October 2012.

Freeman, Nick and Le Bich Ngoc (2007) SME finance in Vietnam: Reviewing past progress and scoping future developments. UNIDO Assistance to Establish the National and Provincial SME Support Infrastructure Working Draft of Technical Report, 12th May. UNIDO_TF/VIE/04/001/11-5X_v3_NJF & LBN.

Gainsborough, Martin (2002) Beneath the veneer of reform: The politics of economic liberalisation in Vietnam. *Communist and Post-Communist Studies* 35, pp. 353–68.

Gainsborough, Martin (2003) Corruption and the politics of economic decentralisation in Vietnam. *Journal of Contemporary Asia* 33(1), pp. 69–84.

Gainsborough, Martin (2009) Privatisation as state advance: Private indirect government in Vietnam. *New Political Economy* 14(2), pp. 257–74.

Gompers, Paul and Josh Lerner (1999) *The venture capital cycle* (Cambridge: MIT Press).

Goodman, John B. and Louis Pauly (1993) The obsolescence of capital controls? *World Politics* 46(1), pp. 50–82.

Groh, Alexzander, Heinrich Liechtenstein and Karsten Lieser (2011) The global venture capital and private equity country attractiveness index: 2011 annual. Available at http://www.wall-street.ro/files/102434-82.pdf, accessed 23 September 2014.

Hung Quoc (2011) Foreign money pouring into hi-tech industries. *The Saigon Times*, 13 April. Available at http://english.thesaigontimes.vn/Home/features/general/16331/, accessed 9 October 2012.

IDG Ventures Vietnam (2007) IDG hosts Vietnam Prime Minister, signs technology agreements. IDG Ventures Vietnam, 30 March. Available at http://idgvv.com.vn/en/press/media/idg-hosts-vietnam-prime-minister-signs-technology-agreements, accessed 20 December 2012.

IntellAsia (2006) Government-backed hi-tech venture capital fund planned. IntellAsia, 9 August. Available at http://www.intellasia.net/government-backed-hi-tech-venture-capital-fund-planned-25294, accessed 20 December 2012.

JICA (Japan International Cooperation Agency)/NEU (National Economic University) (2003) *Vietnam's industrialization strategy in the age of globalization*, 26 May. Available at http://www.grips.ac.jp/forum/module/vietnam/main_en.pdf, accessed 21 August 2014.

Kenney, Martin, Kyonghee Han and Shoko Tanaka (2002) Scattering geese: The venture capital industries of East Asia. A report to the World Bank. BRIE Working Paper 146. Berkeley Roundtable on the International Economy. University of California, Berkeley. Available at http://brie.berkeley.edu/publications/wp146.pdf, accessed 9 October 2012.

Klingler-Vidra Robyn (2014) All politics is local: Sources of variance in the diffusion of venture capital policies. Doctoral thesis, Department of International Relations, London School of Economics and Political Science.

Le, Long S. (2010) Vietnam's endless corruption campaign. *East Asia Forum*, 16 April.

Lenschow, Andrea, Duncan Liefferink and Sietske Veenman (2005) When the birds sing. A framework for analysing domestic factors behind policy convergence. *Journal of European Public Policy* (12)5, pp. 797–816.

Malaysia Venture Capital Management Berhad (2012) Outsource partners: Outsource partners programme. Available at http://www.mavcap.com/Venture-Capital/Outsource-Partners/Outsource-Partners-Programme/, accessed 18 December 2012.

Ministry of Finance (2010) Focusing on economic restructuring and inclusive growth. Available at http://www.mof.gov.vn/portal/page/portal/mof_en/fintegration/gn?pers_id=2420328&item_id=11912133&p_details=1, accessed 9 October 2012.

Ministry of Industry and Trade (2007) Accession of Vietnam to the World Trade Organization. Explanation of Accession Conditions. Available at http://www.mutrap.org.vn/en/library/MUTRAPII/Communicatingpercent20thepercent20Packagepercent20ofpercent20WTOpercent20Committmentspercent20andpercent20Impilcationpercent20topercent20Relevantpercent20Stakeholders.pdf, accessed 9 October 2012.

NVCA (National Venture Capital Association) (2011) Venture impact: The economic importance of venture backed companies to the US economy. IHS Global Insight. Available at http://www.nvca.org/index.php?option=com_content&view=article&id=255&Itemid=103, accessed 9 October 2012.

Nguyen, T.H., Q. Alam, M. Perry and D. Prajogo (2009) The entrepreneurial role of the state and SME growth in Vietnam. *JOAAG* 4(1), pp. 60–71.

Nguyen, Henry (2007) Venture capital and technology industries in Vietnam. IDG Ventures Southeast Asia – Stanford University Events. Available at http://asia.stanford.edu/events/spring07/slides402T/nguyen_slides.pdf, accessed 4 September 2012.

OECD (1996) Venture capital and innovation (Paris: OECD) OCDE/GD(96)168.

OECD (2003) Venture capital: Trends and policy recommendations (Paris: OECD Secretariat Science Technology Industry).

OECD (2011) OECD review of innovation in Southeast Asia: Country profile of innovation: Vietnam.

Ohno, Kenichi (2009) Avoiding the middle income trap: Renovating industrial policy formulation in Vietnam. *ASEAN Economic Bulletin* 26(1), pp. 25–43.

Painter, Martin (2005) The politics of state sector reforms in Vietnam: Contested agendas and uncertain trajectories. *The Journal of Development Studies* 41(2), pp. 261–83.

Perkins, Dwight H. and Vu Thanh Tu Anh (2009) Vietnam's industrial policy: Designing policies for sustainable development. Harvard Kennedy School ASH Institute for Democratic Governance and Innovation. Prepared under UNDP-Harvard Policy Dialogue Papers Series on Vietnam's WTO Accession and International Competitiveness Research. Policy Dialogue Paper Number 1.

Phan, Doan Nam (2003) Institutions and processes in Vietnamese foreign policymaking: Implications for policy towards the United States, in Jonathan R. Stromseth (ed.), *Dialogue on US–Vietnam relations: Domestic dimensions*, pp. 24–29 (San Francisco: The Asia Foundation).

Rogers, Everett M. (1995) *Diffusion of innovations*, 3rd edition (New York: The Free Press).

Sack, Adam and John McKenzie (1998) Establishing a venture capital firm in Vietnam. Private Sector Discussions No. 4. IFC: The Mekong Project Development Facility, Hanoi, Vietnam. Available at http://www.ifc.org/ifcext/mekongpsdf.nsf/AttachmentsByTitle/PSDP+4/$FILE/PSDP-No-4-EN.pdf, accessed 9 October 2012.

Shipan, Charles R. and Craig Volden (2008) The mechanisms of policy diffusion. *American Journal of Political Science* 52(4), pp. 840–57.

Simmons, Beth and Zachary Elkins (2004) The globalization of liberalization: Policy diffusion in the international political economy. *American Political Science Review* 98(1), pp. 171–89.

Simmons, Beth A., Frank Dobbin and Geoffrey Garret (2008) Introduction: The diffusion of liberalization, in Beth A. Simmons, Frank Dobbin and Geoffrey Garret (eds), *The global diffusion of markets and democracy*, pp. 104–40 (Cambridge: Cambridge University Press).

Socialist Republic of Vietnam (2010) Resolution No. 22/NQ-CP of 5 May 2010, on implementation of the Government's Decree No. 56/2009/ ND-CP of June 30, 2009, on support for the development of small- and medium-sized enterprises.

SWF Institute (2012) Recent sovereign wealth fund market size by quarter. SWF Institute. Available at http://www.swfinstitute.org/fund-rankings, accessed 5 December 2012.

Talk Vietnam (2012) Realising SME support policies. VCCI News, 14 May. Available at http://talkvietnam.com/2012/05/realising-sme-support-policies/#.UNLkJeQrWSo, accessed 20 December 2012.

Thoburn, John (2009) Vietnam as a role model for development. UNU-WIDER Research Paper 2009/30. United Nations University. Available at http://www.wider.unu.edu/publications/working-papers/research-papers/2009/en_GB/rp2009-30/, accessed 9 October 2012.

Tran, Tuan Phong (2012) Vietnam's WTO commitments to shape the legal framework for FDI. Vietnam International Law Firm. Available at http://vilaf.com.vn/en/news-a-legal-updates/news/189-vietnams-wto-commitments-to-shape-the-legal-framework-for-fdi-.html, accessed 18 December 2012.

Turley, William S. and Mark Selden (1993) *Reinventing Vietnamese socialism: Doi moi in comparative perspective* (Boulder: Westview Press).

Vu, Xuan Truong (2003) Vietnamese foreign policy and economic renovation, in Jonathan R. Stromseth (ed.), *Dialogue on US-Vietnam relations: Domestic dimensions*, pp. 46–50 (San Francisco: The Asia Foundation).

Whitley, Richard (1992) *Business systems in East Asia* (London: Sage).

World Bank (2006) Overview of the capital markets in Vietnam and directions for development banking finance and investment. Available at http://siteresources.worldbank.org/INTVIETNAM/Resources/Overview_of_the_Capital_Markets_in_Vietnam.pdf, accessed 9 October 2012.
World Bank (2012) Vietnam-World Bank: Long-term companions in development. Report No. 66928. Available at http://documents.worldbank.org/curated/en/2012/01/15823121/vietnam-world-bank-long-term-companions-development, accessed 11 October 2012.
World Trade Organization (2006) Working Party on the Accession of Vietnam Schedule CLX – Viet Nam: Part II – Schedule of Specific Commitments in Services, List of Article II MFN Exemptions. World Trade Organization Working Party on the Accession of Vietnam WT/ACC/VNM/48/Add.2, 27 October. Available at http://www.wto.org/english/news_e/pres06_e/pr455_e.htm, accessed 20 December 2012.
Yeo, Yukyung and Martin Painter (2011) Diffusion, transmutation, and regulatory regime in socialist market economies: Telecoms reform in China and Vietnam. *The Pacific Review* 24(4), pp. 375–95.
Zavatta, Robert (2008) Financing technology entrepreneurs and SMEs in developing countries: Challenges and opportunities: Vietnam country study. InfoDev (World Bank Information for Development Program).

Author Interviews

20 December 2011, Manager in a Vietnam-focused VC fund, Hong Kong.
21 August 2012, International Coordination Division Manager in ASMED, Hanoi.
21 August 2012, ASMED Finance Programs Manager, Hanoi.
22 August 2012, Managing Partner and Founder of Mekong Capital, a Vietnam-based PE/VC management firm, Ho Chi Minh City.
23 August 2012, SME Accelerator Founder and World Bank partner, Ho Chi Minh City.
23 August 2012, Director of Vietnamese fund management firm, Ho Chi Minh City.
24 August 2012, Managing Director of Vietnamese VC management firm and former ICT MNC country manager for Vietnam, Ho Chi Minh City.
24 August 2012, Managing Director of business angel investment firm, Ho Chi Minh City.
24 September 2012, Director of SME Working Group, International Organisation, Singapore.
20 May 2013, ASMED Manager, email exchange.

Financialisation through Microfinance: Civil Society and Market-Building in India

PHILIP MADER

Max Planck Institute for the Study of Societies

Abstract: *Microfinance does not reduce poverty, but it does successfully construct economic relations between owners of capital and borrowers of capital, allowing surpluses to accumulate through finance. It does so by drawing on the agency of financialised civil society actors who facilitate financialisation by working around the state to build new markets in finance and other goods. This article understands financialisation as the expansion of the frontier of financial accumulation. Microfinance is shown to achieve this expansion by establishing credit-based linkages between owners and borrowers of capital, allowing surplus accumulation to take place via the credit relation. Underlying this material relationship, there is also a level at which financialisation motivates and pressures civil society actors to bring microfinance to the poor. By becoming financialised agents themselves, civil society organisations act as conduits for an expansion of financial markets and the construction of new market relations for other goods. A case study of microfinance for water and sanitation in India shows in detail how this construction of markets via civil society works in practice, highlighting the pressures and opportunities presented by microfinance as a vehicle for building markets.*

> Credit is a human right that should be treated as a human right. If credit can be accepted as a human right, then all other human rights will be easier to establish.
>
> Muhammad Yunus (5 April 2011)

> The financialization of microfinance is a relatively small event in the context of a larger world of global finance dominated by foreign exchange markets and the global markets for derivatives. Its symbolic importance, however, is striking.
>
> Aitken (2010, p. 235)

Introduction

Microfinance has held immense appeal in the public imagination, offering a way to ostensibly help poor people escape poverty via the provision of financial services on a for-profit basis. This thoroughly financialised notion of "development" has been inextricably linked with the process of financialisation, as only in a financialised world can slogans such as "Finance For All"[1] or the insistence of Grameen Bank founder and Nobel Peace Prize laureate Muhammad Yunus that "credit is a human right"[2] appear to make any sense.

"Microfinance" refers to the industry of financial institutions that extends a range of services including credit, savings and insurance to people below or near the poverty line in poor countries; an industry in which – recent discursive shifts towards a more encompassing program of "financial inclusion" notwithstanding – credit remains by far the dominant pursuit. It has grown from a niche activity conducted mainly by NGOs in the 1980s into a profitable global industry whose loan portfolio presently surpasses half of total aid.[3] East and South Asia accounted for nearly half (49.5 per cent) of the global microfinance portfolio in 2011, according to the database Mixmarket.

The question asked by this contribution is not "does microfinance work at reducing poverty?" – to which the empirical evidence strongly suggests the answer to be "no" (Banerjee et al., 2010; Bateman, 2010; Duvendack et al., 2011; Hulme, 2007; Karlan and Zinman, 2009) – but rather, "what does microfinance achieve, and how does it work?" The findings here represent a counterpart to Roodman's (2012) suggestion that microfinance's sheer existence is a marker of success, his idea being to evaluate "development as institution building" – the key institutions being those concerned with finance. Instead, the answers proposed in this contribution are twofold. First, microfinance, while according to the best evidence doing nothing to directly reduce material poverty, works at building markets by constructing a credit-based economic relation between owners and borrowers of capital, which facilitates capital accumulation. Second, microfinance does this by drawing on the agency of civil society actors, who perceive credit to be a force for good and therefore act to facilitate such market-building through microfinance.

Microfinance acts as a vehicle for "market-building" – a program that Carroll (2012a, p. 351) describes as an "all-encompassing technocratic agenda being operationalised in the name of development" – at the intersection of the financial sector and civil society. It plays a central role in the pro-market politics of development emerging since the Washington Consensus, which has followed earlier phases of neoliberalism in which first the state's withdrawal from the economy ("roll-back neoliberalism") and subsequently its role as regulatory overseer for the economy ("roll-out neoliberalism") was emphasised. Instead, the new neoliberal politics of development emphasises a drive to actively build markets via a "deep marketisation of development" working on, through and around the state (Carroll, 2012b); a framework on which this paper draws.

In this drive, microfinance helps to construct those institutions that should constitute the actual fabric of market society: multitudes of entrepreneurs, highly competitive enterprises, disciplined borrowers, new financial institutions, and unfettered financial markets. It works *on* the state by requiring a permissive environment for financial services sold at (high) market prices, *through* the state by often employing public development funds, and most importantly also *around* the state by creating new economic institutions and actors to displace and supersede the state's activity. By re-shaping local social and economic relations in ways that accommodate capital channelled through transnational financial markets, microfinance opens up new avenues for capital accumulation via a financialised capital-labour relationship with entrepreneurial, self-exploiting subjects. It thereby shifts the frontier of financial accumulation beyond its present limits into the slum and village economies of the Global South. Moreover, it renders the activities of civil society actors amenable to projects of market-building, with many NGOs increasingly acting as financial institutions. As a case study from India shows, it works even in sectors such as water and sanitation to deploy market-driven "solutions".

The first section of this paper outlines my understanding of financialisation. The following section argues that microfinance materially produces credit relations between owners/intermediaries of capital and borrowers of capital, allowing the former to accumulate surpluses on the labour of the latter. The final section shows that underlying this material relationship is an ideological level of financialisation that motivates and pressures civil society actors to bring microfinance to the poor, with the result that many civil society actors increasingly become conduits for the expansion of financial markets and other market relations. A case study of microfinance for water and sanitation in India shows how such construction of markets via microfinance works in practice, illuminating the forces for market-building at work – part ideological, part practical necessity – and explaining the crucial function of microfinance in this market-building process.

Approaches to Financialisation

Observations on the political and economic significance of "finance capital" and the rentier class go back to the early twentieth century, with Hilferding, Lenin, Kalecki and Keynes analysing a period of financial proliferation that ended in the 1920s and 1930s. The more recent period of resurgent finance was first noted by authors in the late 1970s, with for instance Gramm (1978, p. 309) recognising the expansion of credit as an "alternative to increased wages" for demand stimulation, or later Magdoff and Sweezy (1987, p. 149) describing a "casino economy" on which production increasingly became dependent.

Recent analyses have developed progressively more fine-grained empirical and theoretical explanations, which present five broadly different approaches to financialisation,[4] each emphasising different facets of the whole. Although broad definitions such as Epstein's (2005, p. 3) – "the increasing role of financial motives, financial markets, financial actors and financial institutions in the operation of the domestic and international economies" – are useful, financialisation remains a multidimensional process evading any single definition, and therefore it is worth isolating and exploring separately the different analyses in a brief review.

Financialisation as rising rentier incomes

The political shifts of financial deregulation, monetarism and fiscal austerity since the 1970s substantially increased rentiers' share of economic output – "the income received by owners of financial firms, plus the return to holders of financial assets generally" (Epstein and Jayadev, 2005, p. 49). In the UK, for instance, the inflation-adjusted rentier portion increased approximately 90-fold from the 1960s to the 1990s (Epstein and Jayadev, 2005, p. 56). Since the "rentier class" is an active class, financialisation is a cycle of rentiers using their economic power to shape politics, politics shaping economies in rentiers' interest, and economic outcomes once again increasing rentiers' economic power (Palley, 2008). This process is often driven by financial intermediaries such as investment funds that represent the interests of rentier money – money held by middle classes as well as upper classes, which seeks rent on capital, irrespective of entrepreneurial use – against workers' and entrepreneurs' demands (Deutschmann, 2008a; 2008b). Through changes in the pricing and availability of finance and credit, financial power becomes increasingly concentrated in the hands of rentiers' agents, and contradictions build up as greater returns to capital are demanded and more debt is issued; societies' productive and entrepreneurial base eventually erodes.

Financialisation as a new historical period

Although nearly all analyses of financialisation posit a "then" versus "now" distinction, a specifically historical approach is shared by the *Régulation* School and Social Structures of Accumulation (SSA) theorists, who have explored the differences between the configuration of capitalism in previous periods and the latest period. While an important role for finance is not without historical precedent (Arrighi, 1994), in the view of both schools, financialisation has proven to be a crucial new component of the most recent institutional, regulatory and economic configuration, forming the "neoliberal" variant of capitalism (Wolfson and Kotz, 2010). Technology that encourages financial innovation played a role, but politics and ideology were central to the recent rise of finance (Boyer, 2000; Lipietz, 1992). Supported by the neoliberal creed, the "finance-led growth regime" (Boyer, 2000) of the 1990s and 2000s operated – or still operates – on principles of shareholder value, flexibilisation, inflation control and market supremacy. But while it fixed the problem of profitability that the postwar accumulation regime ran into, "financial hegemony" (Duménil and Lévy, 2011) ultimately led into the present crisis, which both schools agree signals the beginning of a new institutional reconfiguration (Boyer, 2010; McDonough, Reich and Kotz, 2010).

Financialisation as coupon pool capitalism and dis-intermediated finance

A third approach pays greater attention to the magnitude of financial markets and the nature of the financial work done in them (Folkman et al., 2007, pp. 150–62). Froud et al. (2002, p. 120) propose an understanding of financialisation as "coupon pool capitalism", a type of capitalism "where the financial markets are no longer simple intermediaries between household savers and investing firms, but act dynamically to shape the behaviour of both firms and households". The "coupons" are all the different kinds of "financial paper" (primarily bonds and shares) that are traded in the market. Froud et al. (2002) argue that not merely ideas and ideologies (like shareholder value) but the coupon pool itself – the trading of financial paper – has created new pressures and opportunities for households as well as corporations; so that, for instance, "US managers now worry about pressures from the stock market rather than from Japanese competitors" (Froud et al., 2002, p. 135). In this sense, financial markets increasingly exert a power of their own, and if any class of actors is at work, it is the financial managers who seek to restructure companies and economies to match the needs and opportunities of financial investors. In a "Varieties of Capitalism" (VoC) perspective, capitalist countries may adapt to or seek to limit the impacts of this financialisation on their firms and denizens, but they cannot avoid it (Engelen and Konings, 2010).

Financialisation as accumulation through finance

Another approach has understood financialisation in terms of the capital accumulation process increasingly taking place through finance, relative to other activities. Finance, insurance and real estate (FIRE) in the US increased their share in national profits from 11 per cent in the 1950s to nearly 50 per cent in 2001, despite their share in employment remaining stable at between 5 and 7 per cent (Krippner, 2005). Yet financialisation is not a turn away from production as an economic activity, as many presuppose; it is a process whereby finance increasingly becomes the precondition for production. Financialisation then is, so to speak, a shift in where the "magic" in capitalism happens: even firms solidly grounded in goods-production – whose *raison d'être* is producing goods to earn a profit – must increasingly pursue financial activities, with for instance General Electric or Ford now earning half or more of their profits via financial activities (Krippner, 2011, p. 29).

Financialisation as a culture of finance and financial risk

A final approach comes predominantly, though not exclusively, from cultural economy. Rajan (2005; 2010), a macroeconomist, for instance, sees a key cause of financial proliferation and instability in an increasing popular propensity to accept risk, believing it to be calculable and manageable; while in fact many risks are systemic and unpredictable. Technological, regulatory and institutional changes created "financial development" in recent decades and fed a "culture of risk" (Green, 2000). At the individual level, finance creates new roles and identities that are performatively enacted by people and households who come to think of themselves as financial capitalists and risk-takers; a change in ideology. This culture of finance and financial risk takes many forms, from investing through investment clubs (Harrington, 2008); or optimising credit card debts in "the entrepreneurial and calculative management and manipulation of outstanding obligations" (Langley, 2008, p. 141); to a belief in grand visions of a "portfolio society" (Davis, 2009) or "high-risk society" (Mandel, 1996) where success is attained by actively embracing risk. Financialisation is felt in the everyday as a shift in opportunities combined with a change in values and aspirations, whereby the individual becomes its own object of speculation, constantly seeking to fulfil financial opportunity in an increasingly uncertain world (Martin, 2002).

Financialisation is thus a phenomenon approached from different angles, each of which leads to different conclusions about its nature and effects: a reconfiguration of economies benefiting rentiers; a component of the "neoliberal" variant of capitalism; an expansion of the "coupon pool" and a dis-intermediation of finance; a shift to accumulation via finance; and a culture of finance and financial risk. Instead of privileging any particular approach, we should understand financialisation as the sum and interplay of these facets. We see that it is a material phenomenon – a transformation in the composition and functionality of the economy as a productive space – as much as one that operates at the level of ideas and ideologies. Social, political, economic and cultural changes are at work, shaping the ways in which actors use finance, and altering the reach of finance within societies. For the purposes of this research, then, we take financialisation to denote the relatively recent expansion of the frontier of financial accumulation, based on changes in politics, economics, social relations and culture. This not only draws together the above understandings, but also allows us to comprehend microfinance as a force within the expansion of financial markets, pushing the frontier at both the material and ideological levels.

Microfinance-Constructed Credit Relations

In this section and the next we evaluate microfinance as based on its function of expanding credit relations, which pushes the frontier of financial accumulation. The argument is that, beyond facilitating political transformations conducive to financialisation (for instance, by buttressing demands for liberal regulation), microfinance itself works to construct a financialised material relation between the owners of capital and the users of capital, which allows surplus accumulation to take place through finance. This has discernible effects on borrowers, lenders and other actors.

The function of microfinance in facilitating political transformations consistent with neoliberalism, and particularly financial liberalisation, expansion and deepening, has been noted since the turn of the millennium by authors such as Weber (2002, p. 541), who finds that "as a financially steered targeted poverty reduction strategy, microcredit, via its implications for policy, facilitates financial sector liberalisation as well as extending the policy of trade in financial services to the local level". Weber notes that organisations such as the World Bank and the IMF, acting directly as well as through elements such as CGAP,[5] impose an "enabling environment" for financial services "via the microcredit and poverty reduction agenda" and thereby use microfinance to work on the state. Weber theorises the rise of finance in general and microfinance in particular as a form of neoliberal crisis management, arguing: "The implementation of microcredit programmes can be advanced in ways so as to generate implications for financial sector policy restructuring conducive to efforts to advance financial sector liberalisation" (Weber, 2004, p. 360).

This policy function of microfinance working *on* the state (Carroll, 2012b) was most evident in the wake of the Third World debt crisis of the early 1980s, when microcredit was first instituted internationally as an element of development policy. More than 20 years before "privatised Keynesianism" was diagnosed in advanced capitalist economies by Crouch (2009) and Streeck (2011), microfinance deployed under the aegis of Structural Adjustment Plans thus allowed states in the Global South to retreat from such responsibilities as demand management, growth promotion and social welfare, instead letting deregulated financial markets supply low-income people with cheaper credit while traditional industrial labour relations were dismantled. Instead of just being part of neoliberalism, microfinance thereby serves as an active tool in the implementation of neoliberal agendas: reinforcing private authority, entrenching commercial legal frameworks, and curtailing the power of democratic processes to potentially challenge such institutions.

Yet the role of microfinance goes beyond merely acting to advance new economic relations politically in the context of neoliberal transformations: it also increasingly serves to build distinct market-based economic relations of its own, working in particular *around* the state (Carroll, 2012b) to expand and deepen markets. Microfinance, via the credit relations it constructs, creates a material relation between owners of capital, via financial intermediaries, and the sellers of labour-power. The mechanism is the profitability of debt, which – once successfully instituted – makes surplus extraction possible through debt servicing.

This observation is echoed by voices close to the practice of microfinance. Professor Malcolm Harper, co-founder of the erstwhile-leading Indian microfinance institution (MFI) BASIX,[6] voices a fundamental critique of the microfinance sector in what he terms a "tentative Neo-Marxist diagnosis":

> Microfinance offers a more subtle and potentially more durable means whereby those who control capital can exploit those who have only their labour to sell… Microfinanciers can now provide capital, in the form of microcredit, which borrowers use to purchase the tiny amounts of stocks or simple tools they need to run microenterprises. The surplus they can earn is barely sufficient for survival, but because the investments are so small the turnover is relatively high and the borrowers can afford to pay high rates of interest on their loans. Capitalists no longer have to organise and manage labour. They can extract a higher return on their capital not by directly employing people, but by financing their petty businesses under the guise of assisting them to become entrepreneurs. Better still, these entrepreneurs compete against one another rather than combining against capital (Harper, 2011, p. 59).

Harper's observation is contextualised in an evaluation of the stock market flotation of shares in the Mexican MFI Compartamos, which distributed substantial capital returns to management and investors (a number of which were NGOs and civil society organisations, such as ACCION International); but the quoted statement explicitly hypothesises about microfinance in general. Effectively, Harper describes what the *Régulation* and SSA theorists have referred to as the "finance-led growth regime", with a twist. Microfinance is a regime-consistent and regime-furthering means of including – note the recent redefinition of microfinance's purpose as "financial inclusion" – an increasingly individualised, self-employed class of poor people into the mainstream capital accumulation process.

We may wonder why such a system of exploitation is better than employing the poor. After all, it forgoes productive economies of scale that are possible in regular employment situations under Taylorist conditions. Part of the answer is that it offers three distinct advantages to capital-owners. First, it permits the rentier type of accumulation, which requires income streams without actual entrepreneurial activity or innovation on the part of the capital-owner and allows this accumulation to take place at some scale. For instance, India's leading MFI had each loan officer supervise an average of 488 borrowers in 2009 (Mixmarket, 2009b). Hence the entrepreneurial work is outsourced to the individual proletarian labourer who acts as "entreployee" (Voß and Pongratz, 2003). Second, this system avoids major fixed costs for the capital-owner (microloans usually have terms of less than one year) and allows labour power to be acquired on an individual, piece-by-piece basis, with borrowers even self-selecting the most viable routes for surplus-creation available to them under their given conditions. Third, it outsources the largest part of the risk to the borrower, who must (within legal bounds) repay the loans plus 26.6 per cent interest (the global average rate in 2010; author's calculations using Mixmarket yield data), regardless of whether the loan's usage generated a 200 per cent return or a total loss for the borrower. This entrepreneurial risk is kept at a distance from the capital-provider, becoming a mere financial risk that is calculable via average repayment rates and other financial metrics.

For lenders and investors – from high net worth individuals to pension funds or "socially motivated" investors – the system of microfinance offers a potentially high-return/low-risk opportunity for capital accumulation at the present frontier of the global financial market, but borrowers must perform their part by borrowing money and paying a more-than-cost-covering price for it. Money, as Simmel (2004) specified in his *Philosophy of Money*, is a claim on, or entitlement to, the work of others. To lend money therefore means to temporarily transfer those entitlements at the price of a contractual entitlement to a greater magnitude of the borrower's entitlements later; which she, usually, must earn by labour. Therefore, the role of financial markets – including the microfinance market – may be understood as continually creating and mediating new entitlements on the labour of others. As Ingham (2004, p. 12) clarifies, "money is itself a social relation; that is to say, money is a 'claim' or credit that is constituted by social relations that exist independently of the production and exchange of commodities". Conversely, then, to lack money is to be weak in particular social relations, not unproductive or unwilling to exchange.

In microcredit, the lack of sufficient claims to societal wealth – whether for production purposes or social reproduction purposes – among one class of people ("poor people") becomes the basis for a contract with another class able and willing (on certain terms) to rent out capitalist claims. In order to ensure contractual repayment, borrowers have to engage their productive capacities to earn the money for repayment, and then transfer some (or all) of the fruits of their labour to the creditor as a rent on capital. Microfinance, whose central effort is the extension of credit to the poor, is then effectively a form of financial innovation that creates new entitlement relationships between capital-lenders and capital-borrowers, via financial intermediaries, which (like any other credit relation) requires borrowers' discipline in making repayment.

The quintessentially innovative element of microfinance is that this relationship can run directly from the (very) poor to the (very) wealthy, and globally so; literally from Wall Street to the slums and villages of the Global South. If anything, such relationships existed only very indirectly in the past, with diverse layers of middlemen and intermediaries between the owners of substantial amounts of capital and the pawnshops and informal moneylenders who ultimately lent to the poor; or capital-owners had to actually employ the poor in wage-labour relationships. Now, thanks to microfinance, it is possible for a Bill Gates to lend almost directly to an Indian seamstress and hold an entitlement on an asset stream generated by her, with only an MFI in between, which is not to suggest that this is the motivation for Gates' noted support of microfinance, but merely to highlight that the relation materially takes this form. By instituting the technical means for channelling large amounts of capital as loans to people without collateral or assets – means including group lending, social collateral, standardisation and computerisation of disbursement, ratings of MFIs, and the securitisation of microfinance portfolios – the microfinance sector works at creating a more efficient capital-labour relationship, consistent with and conducive to the financialised variant of capitalism.

This raises another question: is the rate of accumulation really so substantial? Premised on informal self-employment of borrowers as much as on their other coping strategies, microfinance operations have in fact upheld very substantial rates of profit accumulation. Even if not always or everywhere, and although punctuated by financialisation-typical crises such as the one in India in 2010 (Mader, 2013), the potential for profits is nevertheless high. For instance, the five largest MFIs in India (the world's biggest microfinance market as of 2009) posted an average ROE[7] from 2005 to 2009 of 36.9 per cent per annum over five years; the provision of investment capital to microfinance in India was an immensely profitable enterprise.[8] Microfinance thereby adds a new dimension to the prevalent system of "accumulation through finance" (Krippner, 2011): it permits – for instance, via the involvement of US-based pension funds such as TIAA-CREF – a process of "financialisation as rising rentier incomes" (Epstein and Jayadev, 2005; Palley, 2008) on the basis of new economic arrangements with the poor. The pre-existing relationship of wealth and poverty between rich and poor transmutes into a financial relationship as the financial frontier is shifted to include ever more borrowers. The persistent rapid growth of the global microfinance loan portfolio – at rates between 27 and 42 per cent each year from 2002 to 2009 (Mixmarket, 2009a) – demonstrates the appeal to capital-owners as much as an unremitting demand for loaned capital, which indicates that few borrowers actually ever "escape" from poverty thanks to microfinance. Rather, the microfinance credit relation appears to be a permanent one, and indeed must be, if microfinance is to remain an attractive investment.

Thanks to microfinance, then, the everyday activities of poverty – the meagre consumption expenditures and micro-entrepreneurial incomes of the poor – enter into modern practices of financial valuation, and are financialised. They are now perceptible and relevant to financial markets, which expand and include them. This reality of mainstream finance entering into the world of poverty is strikingly revealed not least in one of the foremost current publications on poor people's financial lives, *Portfolios of the Poor* (Collins et al., 2009), which compares the aptitude with which poor people manage their money with the work of professional portfolio managers. But the converse message is that microfinance effectively builds portfolios of the poor: through the credit relation, microfinance turns those activities through which the poor manage and survive their poverty into an asset stream that investors can infuse into their portfolios, thereby expanding the "coupon pool" of financial entitlements traded in the market.

Civil Society and Financialisation: The Case of Microfinance for Water and Sanitation

Microfinance has concrete material implications, as the last section showed, but there is an underlying ideological dimension that has guided its ascent. This lies in the changing and malleable social meanings of money and credit, which hinge on the social meanings attributed to the credit relation. The new material relations constructed via microfinance have required agency: the deliberate and inspired actions of civil society actors founded on money's "symbolic qualities generically linked to the ideal of unfettered empowerment" (Dodd, 1994, p. 154) which nurture the notion that loans could promote something greater, such as development, poverty reduction or empowerment. Without having appealed to the "moral sentiments" of many people, without recent decades' processes of financialisation, and without the efforts of diverse "civil society" actors, the growth of microfinance and its attendant construction of new markets could hardly have proceeded in comparable scale and form.

"Civil society" has proven a broad, vague and elusive term; it is taken here as a theorised "third sector", ostensibly beyond the market and the state, populated by non-state, not-for-profit actors, as well as citizens committed to diverse forms of civic engagement. Civil society is a space of societal organisation in the realm between – though not clearly delimitable from – the remits of the state, the market and the private (cf. Kocka, 2000). Despite its effect of facilitating private capital accumulation, and despite its increasing commercialisation and privatisation, the transnational microfinance sector grew and still continues to exist thanks to the efforts of a diverse concoction of actors situated precisely at this intersection of state, market and the private sphere, including but not limited to:

- Microfinance Institutions (MFIs) such as Grameen (Bangladesh) or SEWA (India), which mostly began as (or still are) NGOs or cooperatives;
- International Financial Institutions (IFIs) such as the World Bank acting as funders, standardisers, political promoters and resource bases for MFIs;
- governmental development agencies and multilateral funding bodies such as USAID or IFAD (International Fund for Agricultural Development);
- special transnational non-state non-profit organisations such as ACCION or Kiva, funding microfinance but often also acting as think-tanks and advocacy bodies;
- philanthropic funds and foundations such as Oxfam or CARE International;
- private wealthy individuals who fund and prominently promote microfinance;
- banks and other for-profit financial institutions, funding or channelling funds from large investors or retail investors (often "socially motivated");
- specialised investment funds; and
- a broader social movement committed to the idea and practice of microfinance.

States, market actors and private individuals (entrepreneurs, investors) interpenetrate here with the realm of classical civil society actors, forming what Aitken (2010) terms the "ambiguous incorporations" of microfinance.

Strikingly, under the rubric of poverty reduction and development, these actors have come together to construct a for-profit financial subsector that is increasingly linked to mainstream financial circuits (cf. Dieckmann, 2007); a deliberate act of market-building working *through* (with the involvement of public funders) and *around* the state, as well as *on* it. Of crucial importance as an explanatory factor here is the fifth and most underexplored facet of financialisation, the "culture of finance and financial risk", which – we saw earlier – creates new roles and identities that are performatively enacted by actors who come to think of themselves as capitalists and risk-takers. Authors such as Bajde (2013, p. 2), for instance, locate the culture of microfinance in a "utopian ideology of entrepreneurial philanthropy", knitted together at the intersection of the market and charity, although "rife with ideological frictions". With reference to the users of the online microlending platform Kiva, Bajde traces how small-scale microfinance funders seek to "implement their moral visions of 'good society'" through finance-based rather than giving-based acts of philanthropy (Bajde, 2013, p. 4). Kiva lenders identify with "their" borrowers' entrepreneurialism, treating "the loan as an affirmation of their personal moral beliefs". This allows, as Kiva co-founder Jessica Jackley puts it, "the average individual to feel like a mini-Bill Gates by building a portfolio of investments in businesses around the globe" (cited in Bajde, 2013, p. 9), creating the new identity of the charitable small investor, using and shaping transnational financial markets in the pursuit of social aims.

Lofty motives notwithstanding, this market-building requires a specific form of financial "governmentality" – an insidious form of authority that contributes to the "transformation of microlending into a fully financialized object" (Aitken, 2010, p. 232), and works to instil market discipline among actors and realms that have regularly evaded market forces. The re-framing of for-profit credit as a socially-necessary intervention constitutes a re-framing of credit itself as a socially-necessary good, which Aitken argues makes finance recognisable no longer as a contestable or dubious construct, but rather as a rational and universally useful tool. For Young (2010, p. 607), microfinance thereby serves to strategically reposition places and people "in relation to the perceived opportunities or risks they present to global capital flows". Financial flows and the associated practices are "geopolitical technologies" that generate new social roles and identities, and restructure the activities of civil society actors. From the philanthropist or "social investor" via the developmental NGO to the beneficiary herself, participants in this financial chain are asked to think of themselves as capitalists and risk-takers, channelling market forces towards the aim of promoting development. By acquiring new meanings – as socially necessary and benevolent – the rules of mainstream finance, which include regular repayment schedules, monitoring, and a drive for profitability, enter into developmental activities previously considered the remit of NGOs and civil society.

Case: Microfinance for water and sanitation in India

The expansion of credit relationships through microfinance has had even further-reaching effects. Not only does microfinance in general shift the frontier of financial accumulation, concomitantly increasing the amount of market labour poor people must perform for loan repayment; it also increasingly serves to marketise other goods through novel projects emerging from the realm of civil society. This is directly related to the changing social meaning of credit under financialisation, whereby credit is now held as a rational, necessary and empowering tool for producing social good. Thanks to microfinance, the need among poor people for the means of social reproduction such as water and sanitation (and other public goods; see Mader, 2011a) also becomes increasingly recognisable to financial markets as a financial need, to be remedied via the construction of markets in finance. Actors associated with civil society play a key part in this process, as the case of a project using microfinance for water and sanitation in India shows.

The concept of microfinance for water and sanitation – that is, the application of credit to certain goods that constitute elementary means of social reproduction – has existed for over 15 years. As Reis and Mollinga (2009, p. 3) explain: "Due to the finance gap in the RWSS[9] sector and the paradigm of cost-recovery, microcredit schemes have globally become a popular element of RWSS policies in recent years"; also increasingly in urban areas, as India shows. Between January and July 2010, I performed field research on a project whose purpose was to channel microfinance funding into the provision of water and sanitation to slum households in several urban and peri-urban areas of Andhra Pradesh (AP), India.

The organisational structure of the project in AP consisted substantially of three organisations: a philanthropic foundation managed by a very rich North American IT entrepreneur ("the Foundation"); an India-based NGO working with women's groups in slums ("the NGO"); and an India-based development consultancy founded by a microfinance investment fund manager ("the Consultants").[10] The project consisted of three interventions: (1) microfinance-funded household water tap connections; (2) microfinance-funded sanitary latrines; and (3) pay-per-can drinking water from reverse osmosis (RO) purification plants – the latter having no direct microfinance element. The tap connections and latrines were supposed to be funded by women using microfinance loans. A subsidy from the Foundation, disbursed by the NGO, was supposed to cover 50 per cent of the notional cost (which was estimated by many recipients to be an understatement of the real cost), while the remainder of the funds were to be borrowed by households from microfinance providers of their choice. While the outcomes of the project itself were politically as well as economically problematic as explained in Mader (2011b), I turn here to evaluating the roles played by the three organisations involved.

At the apex of the project sat *the Foundation*, whose strategic decisions were taken at head offices in the US, while operations were managed from India. The project was part of its "Family Economic Stability" program, described as supporting "institutions that offer impoverished urban families access to the capital they need to put their children on the path to self-sufficiency", which in practice consisted mostly of grants to and equity investments in urban MFIs – evidently a rather narrow definition of "family economic stability". Relative to its overall microfinance support, the sum disbursed as a grant of just under US$1 million for the latrine and water tap subsidies was fairly minor. The Foundation's India-based staff were kept up to date by the NGO on the progress of the subsidy disbursement, which was far slower than intended, because only a fraction of households actually came forward. The Foundation did not take any further active role in implementing or steering the project, but hired the Consultants (more below) to monitor the activities of the NGO and evaluate the project's impact.

The NGO, the implementing agency of the project, had just under one decade of experience in working with women's groups, mainly on "capacity building" for Self-Help Groups (SHGs) in the context of the Andhra Pradesh government's bank linkage program. It was respected and well known in civil society circles, and well connected with regional governmental bodies while retaining independence. Its employees – mostly trained social workers – were responsible in the project for disbursing subsidy money to the women for the construction of water and sanitation facilities; disbursement was contingent on progress with construction. As "capacity builders", the employees also played a crucial role in facilitating women's access to additional loan finance, via the SHG-bank linkage and other microfinance. Around the time the water and sanitation project was being rolled out, federations of SHGs (representing up to around 200 individuals) were upgraded as formal "cooperative societies" whose income statements were subject to a formal financial accounting audit; through a successful audit it was hoped that federations would be able to gain easier and cheaper access to financial services from the formal financial market.

In practice, the NGO's (mostly male) employees functioned as local project coordinators, training providers, informal financial auditors[11] and, whenever considered necessary, financial and social discipliners (vis-à-vis all-women SHG members). They regularly coordinated with municipal officials, sometimes attempting to facilitate construction of network infrastructure in certain neighbourhoods, but they could only rarely secure such public investments. As officials explained in multiple interviews, the municipalities themselves lacked resources, while the loan finance and subsidy, crucially, were directed towards the end users – with the result that the constructed water and sanitation systems often lacked the underlying public infrastructure necessary for proper functioning. For the NGO, the identified problem was water and sanitation, and the identified solution in the project – for pragmatic reasons, given the conditions of the Foundation – was to facilitate microfinance. As the NGO's project director explained in an interview, the microfinance-based setup was chosen for two reasons – first to prevent a possible corrupt misallocation of funds (if larger volumes were disbursed via political channels), and second because microfinance was plentifully available and the Foundation wanted to support this: "Microfinance, microfinance is the requirement. The finance is small, micro".

The third group, the *Consultants*, proved a fascinating team to work with and study as participant-observer. Consisting mostly of internationally-mobile Indian-born MBAs without an engineering or development background, the team had been hired to design an impact evaluation[12] of the water and sanitation project in the slums (slums they visited only rarely, briefly, and generally rather unwillingly). On the side, the Consultants were seeking to use the Foundation-funded evaluation to improve their own "knowledge base" for future "BOP" ("bottom of the pyramid") water and sanitation interventions using microfinance, which they would later sell as consulting expertise or as completed business models to other civil society and corporate entities. The consulting company had been founded as a (*de jure* independent) pet project by its boss, a venture capital microfinance fund manager, and its role was effectively to act as a highly visible think-tank for market-driven "social business" solutions to problems at the "BOP", producing conducive policy recommendations as well as private sector consulting services while remaining separate from the more traditional venture capital fund located in another city.

Microfinance was understood by the Consultants to represent a uniquely "demand-driven solution", and demand for water and sanitation projects was always premised on *financial* improvements from better facilities. The assumption was that the poor would recognise financial benefits and therefore spend money on water and sanitation improvements, since realistically in no other way could a market-driven solution to the problem have been espoused. That the poor were not coming forward in droves did not seem to irritate the team leader, who explained: "We know better. It's not that the demand isn't there, it's just that they don't know better". A commonly-used term therefore was "latent demand", which would take "cultural change" to finally become "real" demand for a for-profit business model. In report-writing (the main activity of the consultants) the concept of "need" was consistently translated into "market potential", the "poor" were termed "BOP segment" (of the market), and to "use" or "employ" any device (or person) was to "leverage" it (or them) – financial terminology and logics routinely pervaded many formal utterances of thought.

The NGO's project director once expressed the difference between his NGO's ethos and the Consultants' mode of thought in a private moment: "They are corporate. So of course they will see things in a corporate way" – where the NGO saw social problems, the Consultants saw market potential. Whenever project proposals and reports were being written by the Consultants, the premise from the outset – never a finding in the end – was that some way must be found for the private sector to finance a proposed intervention, which in turn required the poor themselves to pay. Yet since no market was present to service the needs of the poor, the appropriate technologies and actors for the formation of a market had to be introduced, and thereby the market built. Furthermore, since the sheer poverty of the "BOP segment" represented a problem in making the poor pay for market-driven solutions, it was suggested that the poor could borrow the money, and therefore microfinance was the solution for market-building in water and sanitation.

In this project using microfinance for water and sanitation in India, market-building to address social problems was for each actor involved in different ways a matter of practical-pragmatic as well as ideological necessity. Microfinance served as a market-compatible means for addressing social problems, acting as a tool for building new markets in the means of social reproduction such as water and sanitation. For the Foundation, building a market via microfinance was its way to promote "family economic stability"; for the NGO, microfinance was a requirement for gaining funds to address an urgent problem; for the Consultants, microfinance was the only conceivable way of extracting "demand" from the poor for their market-based "solutions". The financial presence of the amply-funded microfinance sector was acutely felt by all actors, and differently interpreted respectively by the NGO, the Consultants and the Foundation; in part as an opportunity to cooperate, in part as sheer necessity. The Consultants, far more than the NGO (which worked closer to the life-reality of the intended beneficiaries, and retained some scepticism), were palpably permeated by a "culture of finance", in which all problems were simply a matter of "leveraging" the adequate financial resources. That this should effectively mean building financial markets around goods such as water and sanitation, whose status as marketable goods was simply assumed, was an unquestionable inevitability. For the NGO, this was a pragmatic (and mostly unquestioned) necessity resulting from the acute pressure to gain funds, as well as scepticism of the state as a means of delivery. For the Foundation, the specific reasons why it sought to promote "family economic stability" via microfinance remained unclear.

As the case in India shows, microfinance's market-building potential reaches beyond its intrinsic function of coaxing market-oriented labour from borrowers for repayment, through which microfinance extends financial market linkages into new realms so that mainstream capital accumulation circuits now reach many slums and villages in the Global South. Microfinance, we see, also increasingly pervades the activities and strategies of actors associated with civil society in areas traditionally unrelated to financial markets, making these actors conduits for a broader, more comprehensive, market-building project. In the case of water and sanitation, the spread of microfinance has opened new and perhaps surprising channels for projects of market-building, whereby microfinance serves as a tool to operate around the state for an expansion and deepening of financial market linkages. The Indian case reveals how microfinance generates a perceived urgency for addressing social problems through expanding and deepening markets for finance, and how some civil society actors, in this sense, have become agents for building markets even in the means of social reproduction such as water and sanitation. This process repositions NGOs as purveyors of market-based solutions to social problems – partly out of pragmatic necessity, and partly inspired by ideology – and poor people as consumers.

Conclusion

This paper has discussed five different approaches to financialisation, finding it to be an expansion of the frontier of financial accumulation based on changes in politics, economics, social relations and culture. Microfinance is part of this expansion of the frontier of financial accumulation, creating new channels for surplus accumulation with an increasingly individualised, self-employed class of labourers; yet it has drawn on normative and ideological shifts that present finance as a means for positive social ends. The paper has thereby integrated a study of the distinct material effects of microfinance, which are to create asset streams that allow rentiers to accumulate capital on the basis of the labour power of the poor, with a study of how these material effects hinge on changes in the social meaning assigned to credit. Moreover, the paper has demonstrated how this shift in the frontier of financial accumulation engages civil society actors in promoting the expansion of credit markets, even in areas seemingly unrelated to credit, such as water and sanitation in India.

The case study of a project linking access to water and sanitation with microfinance in India demonstrates how microfinance, in the context of the larger global process of financialisation, has mobilised civil society actors as agents for building markets in the means of social reproduction. The ostensibly apolitical financial nexus can actively serve the project of building markets in goods such as water and sanitation, whose politically-engineered privatisation encountered fierce political resistance during the 1980s and 1990s. We may interpret this as a process of marketisation and micro-privatisation through the back door, via finance, which is fully congruent with the vision espoused by the father figure of microfinance: "government, as we now know it, should pull out of most things except for law enforcement, the justice system, national defense, and foreign policy, and let the private sector … take over its other functions" (Yunus, 2003, p. 204). This vision's logical conclusion clarifies the increasingly important role of financial markets and financial actors in projects of market-building. Weber (2002; 2004) highlights how microfinance has always been a political tool for market-building by working on the state, so this finding should not be a complete surprise. This article considers a different dimension and shows that microfinance should also be recognised as a tool for market-building by working around the state – as part of the new neoliberal politics of development in which development efforts directly work to open up new capital accumulation avenues. By deploying market-driven "solutions" to problems of global poverty, while not succeeding in reducing this poverty, microfinance evidently *is* working to construct institutions of a market society, in particular the financial institutions that actively re-shape social relations in ways conducive to capital accumulation.

Acknowledgments

I am indebted to two anonymous reviewers for their highly valuable comments, as well as the participants and organisers of the Workshop on 'Citizens, Civil Society and the Politics of "Building Markets" in Asia' held at the Lee Kuan Yew School of Public Policy, National University of Singapore, in February 2012, particularly Toby Carroll, Darryl Jarvis and Heloise Weber.

Notes

1. Title of an academic business magazine issue (Werner, 2012).
2. Credit, following Yunus, even being a more fundamental right than others. Just how problematic this notion is evidently does not occur to Yunus or other microfinance enthusiasts. As Thomas Dichter cogently points out in the award-winning documentary *The Micro Debt*: "Muhammad Yunus said that credit is a Human Right; but he never said that debt is a Human Right" (Heinemann, 2010).
3. The four largest donors posted a development assistance budget of US$63,230 million in 2009, contributing more than half of all DAC-registered foreign aid (OECD, 2010). Microfinance loans amounted to US$72 billion. These budgets furthermore partially include an unknown amount of government and multilateral support for microfinance programs, registered as aid.
4. Other authors have categorised and grouped the literature differently. The works of different authors are grouped here not by authors' affiliations or convictions, but by their shared *objects* of interest. The approaches are not mutually exclusive; nor have the authors necessarily focused exclusively on the approach they are associated with here. Merely to highlight the dimensions of financialisation systematically we distinguish the different foci.
5. Consultative Group to Assist the Poor; a multi-donor organisation founded by and housed within the World Bank.
6. BASIX was the Indian sector leader for many years.
7. Mixmarket (2009b). ROE = Return on Equity. Author's calculation using Mixmarket data to determine a 5-year weighted average for the five largest MFIs in India as of 2009: SKS, Spandana, Share, Bandhan and AML.
8. Comparing these figures to, for instance, an overall RoE of all US firms (15.2 per cent in 2008 and 9.9 in 2009), or 7.2 and minus 69.0 per cent in US financial services (in 2008 and 2009 respectively) (Damodaran, 2011), the extent to which Indian MFIs were lucrative is evident – especially given their reputation at the time of being virtually risk-free, thanks to the sector's average loan repayment rate of more than 99 per cent. The crisis of 2010, of course, changed this.
9. RWSS = Rural water supply and sanitation.
10. The identities of these organisations and their members have been kept anonymous here, due in part to an agreement with one of the organisations, and there is no intention to affect their reputations in any way. The background, methods and findings of this research from a public goods-theoretic perspective are reported in Mader (2011a).
11. Preparing the books in advance to the chartered accountants performing the formal audit.
12. The impact evaluation questionnaire, developed by the author as stipulated by the Consultants, regrettably was never implemented beyond test stage. To the best of my knowledge, no systematic impact evaluation was ever performed, and none may ever have been intended for the final report to the Foundation.

References

Aitken, Rob (2010) Ambiguous incorporations: Microfinance and global governmentality. *Global Networks* 10(2), pp. 223–43.

Arrighi, Giovanni (1994) *The long twentieth century* (London: Verso).

Bajde, Domen (2013) "Marketized" philanthropy: Mapping Kiva's utopian ideology of entrepreneurial philanthropy. *Marketing Theory*, 16 January. doi:10.1177/1470593112467265.

Banerjee, Abhijit, Esther Duflo, Rachel Glennerster and Cynthia Kinnan (2010) The miracle of microfinance? Evidence from a randomized evaluation. Unpublished paper, 30 June. Cambridge, MA.

Bateman, Milford (2010) *Why doesn't microfinance work?* (London: Zed Books).

Boyer, R. (2000) Is a finance-led growth regime a viable alternative to Fordism? A preliminary analysis. *Economy and Society* 29(1), pp. 111–45.

Boyer, Robert (2010) How new will the next regulatory regime be? *Socio-Economic Review* 8(3), pp. 541–47.

Carroll, Toby (2012a) Introduction: Neo-liberal development policy in Asia beyond the post Washington Consensus. *Journal of Contemporary Asia* 42(3), pp. 350–58.

Carroll, Toby (2012b) Working on, through and around the state: The deep marketisation of development in the Asia-Pacific. *Journal of Contemporary Asia* 42(3), pp. 378–404.

Collins, Daryl, Jonathan Morduch, Stuart Rutherford and Orlanda Ruthven (2009) *Portfolios of the poor: How the world's poor live on $2 a day* (Princeton, NJ: Princeton University Press).

Crouch, Colin (2009) Privatised Keynesianism: An unacknowledged policy regime. *The British Journal of Politics and International Relations* 11(3), pp. 382–99.

Damodaran, Aswath (2011) The data page. *Useful Data Sets*. Available at http://people.stern.nyu.edu/adamodar/New_Home_Page/data.html, accessed 3 May 2012.

Davis, Gerald F. (2009) *Managed by the markets: How finance re-shaped America* (Oxford: Oxford University Press).

Deutschmann, Christoph (2008a) Der kollektive „Buddenbrooks-Effekt": Die Finanzmärkte und die Mittelschichten. *MPIfG Discussion Paper* 08(5), pp. 1–21.

Deutschmann, Christoph (2008b) *Kapitalistische Dynamik: Eine gesellschaftstheoretische Perspektive* (Wiesbaden: VS Verlag für Sozialwissenschaften).

Devarajan, P. (2005) Tread warily on MFI loans; but spare a thought for rural poor. *The Hindu Business Line*, 1 October.

Dieckmann, Raimar (2007) Microfinance: An emerging investment opportunity. *Deutsche Bank Research Current Issues*, 19 December.

Dodd, Nigel (1994) *The sociology of money: Economics, reason and contemporary society* (Cambridge: Polity Press).

Duménil, Gérard and Dominique Lévy (2011) *The crisis of neoliberalism* (Cambridge, MA: Harvard University Press).

Duvendack, Maren, Richard Palmer-Jones, James G. Copestake, Lee Hooper, Yoon Loke and Nitya Rao (2011) *Systematic review: What is the evidence of the impact of microfinance on the well-being of poor people?* (London: EPPI Centre, Social Science Research Unit, Institute of Education, University of London).

Engelen, Ewald and Martijn Konings (2010) Financial capitalism resurgent: Comparative institutionalism and the challenges of financialization, in R. Whitley, O.K. Pedersen, C. Crouch, J.L. Campbell and G. Morgan (eds), *The Oxford handbook of comparative institutional analysis*, pp. 601–24 (Oxford: Oxford University Press).

Epstein, Gerald A., ed. (2005) *Financialization and the world economy* (Northampton, MA: Edward Elgar Publishing).

Epstein, Gerald A. and Arjun Jayadev (2005) The rise of rentier incomes in OECD countries: Financialization, central bank policy and labor solidarity, in G.A. Epstein (ed.), *Financialization and the world economy*, pp. 46–74 (Northampton, MA: Edward Elgar Publishing).

Folkman, Peter, Julie Froud, Sukhdev Johal and Karel Williams (2007) Intermediaries (or another Group of Agents?), in I. Erturk, J. Froud, S. Johal, A. Leaver and K. Williams (eds), *Financialization at work*, pp. 150–61 (London: Routledge).

Froud, Julie, Sukhdev Johal and Karel Williams (2002) Financialisation and the coupon pool. *Capital and Class* 26(3), pp. 119–51. doi:10.1177/030981680207800106.

Gramm, Warren S. (1978) Credit saturation, secular redistribution, and long-run stability. *Journal of Economic Issues* 12(2), pp. 307–27.

Green, S. (2000) Negotiating with the future: The culture of modern risk in global financial markets. *Environment and Planning D: Society and Space* 18(1), pp. 77–89.

Harper, Malcolm (2011) The commercialization of microfinance: Resolution or extension of poverty, in M. Bateman (ed.), *Confronting microfinance: Undermining sustainable development*, pp. 49–63 (Sterling, VA: Kumarian Press).

Harrington, Brooke (2008) *Pop finance: Investment clubs and the new investor populism* (Princeton, NJ: Princeton University Press).

Heinemann, Tom (2010) *The micro debt: A critical investigation into the dark side of microcredit*. TV Documentary, NRK/Brennpunkt (Oslo: DR Sales).

Hulme, David (2007) Is microdebt good for poor people? A note on the dark side of microfinance, in T. Dichter and M. Harper (eds), *What's wrong with microfinance?*, pp. 19–22 (Bourton on Dunsmore: Immediate Technology Publications).

Ingham, Geoffrey (2004) *The nature of money* (Cambridge: Polity Press).

Karlan, Dean and Jonathan Zinman (2009) Expanding microenterprise credit access: Using randomized supply decisions to estimate the impacts in Manila. *Yale Economics Department Working Paper No. 68 / Yale University Economic Growth Center Discussion Paper No. 976.*

Kocka, Jürgen (2000) Zivilgesellschaft als historisches Problem und Versprechen, in M. Hildermeier, J. Kocka and C. Conrad (eds), *Europäische Zivilgesellschaft in Ost und West: Begriff, Geschichte, Chancen*, pp. 13–39 (Frankfurt/Main: Campus).

Krippner, Greta (2005) The financialization of the American economy. *Socio-Economic Review* 3(2), pp. 173–208.

Krippner, Greta (2011) *Capitalizing on crisis: The political origins of the rise of finance* (Cambridge, MA: Harvard University Press).

Langley, Paul (2008) Financialization and the consumer credit boom. *Competition and Change* 12(2), pp. 133–47.

Lipietz, Alain (1992) *Towards a New Economic Order: Postfordism, ecology and democracy* (Oxford: Oxford University Press).

Mader, Philip (2011a) Attempting the production of public goods through microfinance: The case of water and sanitation. *Journal of Infrastructure Development* 3(2), pp. 153–70.

Mader, Philip (2011b) Making the poor pay for public goods via microfinance: Economic and political pitfalls in the case of water and sanitation. *MPIfG Discussion Paper* 11(14).

Mader, Philip (2013) Rise and fall of microfinance in India: The Andhra Pradesh crisis in perspective. *Strategic Change* 22(1–2), pp. 47–65.

Magdoff, Harry and Paul Sweezy (1987) *Stagnation and the financial explosion* (New York: Monthly Review Press).

Mandel, Michael (1996) *The high-risk society: Peril and promise in the new economy* (New York City: Crown Business).

Martin, Randy (2002) *Financialization of daily life* (Philadelphia: Temple University Press).

McDonough, Terrence, Michael Reich and David M. Kotz (2010) Introduction: Social structure of accumulation theory for the 21st century, in T. McDonough, M. Reich and D.M. Kotz (eds), *Contemporary capitalism and its crises: Social structure of accumulation theory for the 21st century*, pp. 1–19 (Cambridge: Cambridge University Press).

Mixmarket (2009a) Microfinance at a glance. Available at http://www.mixmarket.org/, accessed 3 May 2012.

Mixmarket (2009b) Microfinance in India. Available at http://www.mixmarket.org/mfi/country/India, accessed 4 December 2011.

OECD (2010) Statistical Annex of the 2010 Development Co-operation Report, Table 1. Available at http://www.oecd.org/dac/stats/dac/dcrannex, accessed 27 November 2010.

Palley, Thomas I. (2008) *Financialization: What it is and why it matters* (IMK at the Hans Boeckler Foundation, Macroeconomic Policy Institute).

Rajan, Raghuram (2005) Has financial development made the world riskier? Paper presented at The Greenspan Era: Lessons for the Future Federal Reserve Bank of Kansas Symposium, Jackson Hole, Wyoming.

Rajan, Raghuram (2010) *Fault lines: How hidden fractures still threaten the world economy* (Princeton: Princeton University Press).

Reis, Nadine and Peter Mollinga (2009) Microcredit for rural water supply and sanitation in the Mekong Delta: Policy implementation between the needs for clean water and "beautiful latrines". *ZEF Working Paper 49*, Center for Development Research ZEF, Bonn.

Roodman, David (2012) *Due diligence* (Baltimore, MD: Brookings Institution Press).

Simmel, Georg (2004) *The philosophy of money* (London: Routledge).

Streeck, Wolfgang (2011) The crises of democratic capitalism. *New Left Review* 71, September–October, pp. 5–29.

Voß, G. Günter and Hans J. Pongratz (2003) From employee to "entreployee" – towards a "self-entrepreneurial" work force? *Concepts and Transformation* 8, pp. 239–54.

Weber, Heloise (2002) The imposition of a global development architecture: The example of microcredit. *Review of International Studies* 28(3), pp. 537–55.

Weber, Heloise (2004) The "new economy" and social risk: Banking on the poor? *Review of International Political Economy* 11(2), pp. 356–86.

Werner, Angelika (2012) Finance for all – Zur Zukunft der Mikrofinanz. *Sonnemann Business Magazine – Frankfurt School of Finance and Management* 8, p. 82.

Wolfson, Martin H. and David M. Kotz (2010) A reconceptualization of social structure of accumulation theory, in T. McDonough, M. Reich and D.M. Kotz (eds), *Contemporary capitalism and its crises: Social structure of accumulation theory for the 21st century*, pp. 72–90 (Cambridge: Cambridge University Press).

Young, Stephen (2010) Gender, mobility and the financialisation of development. *Geopolitics* 15(3), pp. 606–27.

Yunus, Muhammad (2003) *Banker to the poor: Micro-lending and the battle against world poverty* (New York: PublicAffairs).

Yunus, Muhammad (2011) Facebook post, 5 April. Available at https://www.facebook.com/Dr.M.Yunus/posts/175581065825456, accessed 8 September 2014.

Market Creation by Leninist Means: The Regulation of Financial Services in the People's Republic of China

NEIL COLLINS

Nazarbayev University, Kazakhstan

JOERN-CARSTEN GOTTWALD

Ruhr University Bochum, Germany

Abstract: *Within the process of China's transition from a centrally-administered to a more market-oriented economy, financial services have played a very special role, but in a counter-intuitive way: what looks like Western market economics turns out to be a Leninist regulatory model. Even as international financial service providers and regulatory communities are invited to play a role in the creation of a Chinese market in financial services, the Communist Party has strengthened its control of top personnel, the judiciary and the media. The reform of the central bank and the establishment of technically independent regulatory agencies seemed to have taken China down the path of OECD economies. The model of a very specific post-regulatory state with Chinese characteristics, however, has not fully incorporated the notion of private authority. Such an acceptance would pose a threat to the CCP monopoly on political power. The attempt to use only semi-private organisations to develop financial markets undermines the long-term stability of the political and economic order.*

Introduction

> ...the whole point of a Leninist-style party is that it should take decisions and act in the name of the people, and should possess sovereign authority in doing so (Porter, 2011, p. 121).

For the Communist Party of China (CCP), the mechanisms of the state are a veneer for party control. Market and associated regulatory institutions are tested and calibrated by their usefulness to the party-state's central purposes. Given the scale, complexity and lack of clarity associated with Chinese economic and social development, however, the instruments to achieve the party-state's objectives are not always easily identified or devised. In many areas of policy, therefore, China presents a paradox of conformity and confusion. This paper seeks to explore the creation of a market in financial services through the gradual development of a regulatory regime by using "Leninist means" (Heilmann, 2005) in order to illustrate the pervasive and persistent relationship between Leninist means and "socialist market" ends. It will show that the Chinese state shares with others the imperative to appear to be adhering to global standards in its regulatory regime but that, when these clash with party priorities, local considerations triumph. Indeed, this paper takes as its understanding of a Leninist state that it successfully defines its autonomy from other social and economic forces to a degree unmatched in most other models.

The financial and economic crisis that erupted in the United States in 2008 shines a light on the Janus-head nature of financial markets: they are the key to economic growth and development in open-market economies, but their capacity for socioeconomic destruction cannot be ignored.

The world has grown accustomed to crises originating from financial instabilities in emerging markets. In 2008, proponents of the idea of never-ending beneficial financial innovation in Western de-regulated capitalisms had to learn the hard way that their preferred models were also susceptible to failure. In the wake of the current global financial crisis, some enthusiasts' eyes have turned to the People's Republic of China (PRC) as a hopeful alternative. China has been much less – or, at least, very differently – affected by the global crisis, but even this shift in public interest has proven to be problematic. This development has simply highlighted and deepened the gap between China analysis offered by experts in global politics and that which is offered by specialist China-watchers: while the former discuss the impact of China's unstoppable "rise", the latter are raising serious issues about the stability of China's financial system.

In this paper, we argue that the Leninist-style introduction of market reforms has created a very specific post-regulatory state with Chinese characteristics (Tsai and Dean, 2013). The policies of market creation adopted by the leadership of the CCP followed the rationale of preserving its dominant position in Chinese politics. On an individual level, this allowed top representatives of the party-state to pursue business opportunities. On a collective level, it provided the ground for a much more efficient and comprehensive utilisation of Chinese and foreign savings for the unqualified pursuit of economic growth. Reform of the financial sector was closely tied to the reform of the state-owned enterprise system and was deferred to a relatively late moment in China's opening up. Once it was being approached with zeal – which was in the late 1990s, by the Zhu Rongji government – it followed the basic path of attempting to outgrow its inefficiencies and structural problems (Huang et al., 2005). This strategy preserved some old structural flaws, such as political meddling in management issues, and created new issues, such as the turf wars between various administrative systems. In general, therefore, the policies of market creation in the financial sector did not follow the logic of creating an optimum framework for a maturing market economy but, rather, pursued two very different and seemingly contradictory objectives:

- maintaining Leninist control of a key sector of the economy; and
- giving foreign and domestic capital better access to the Chinese business sector.

These policies have been successful in preserving growth rates, even under the severe conditions of the 2008 crisis, but this has been achieved while the underpinnings of the Chinese financial system have continued to weaken. In this paper, we provide an analysis of the policies of market creation by the Chinese leadership by regarding them as an attempt to integrate a regulatory state model into the structures of a Leninist party-state.

Following earlier works by, among others, Heilmann (2005), Pearson (2005; 2007; 2011), Schlichting (2008; 2009) and Yeo and Painter (2011), we revisit the process and outcomes of China's regulatory reforms in the light of the current global crisis. In a political context, it is unclear whether positive developments in the markets will impact encouragingly on the broadening of reforms. We examine the improved foundations for capital markets and the gradual opening to external actors (Herd et. al., 2010). These developments stand alongside continuing issues in corporate governance and politicised selection of issuing companies. Adopting the analytical perspective of regulatory capitalism we respect the variety of forms of governance and regulation within a national economy (Levi-Faur and Jordana, 2005). As Rosalyn Hsueh put it, "the Chinese state has pursued a *liberalization two-step* [sic]. It has shifted from universal controls on FDI and private industry on the aggregate level across all industries to selective controls at the sectoral level" (Hsueh, 2011, p. 3). We express our doubts that the specific reform path the Chinese authorities have taken in the area of financial services constitutes a model to be followed by other nations and, therefore, question the validity of widespread expectations that China will become a major source of future global regulation. If the question is posed as to how far Western "efficiency based" models of analysis properly reflect China's uniqueness (Maswana, 2008), we argue that debates on China's political economy – including the one on the "China model" – need to take into account the diversity of regulatory regimes within the Chinese economy.[1]

The fundamental questions about the abatement of direct party-state interference have not been answered. How and how far can the CCP stand back from the financial markets? Indeed, current speculation leaves room for frightening scenarios of doom (Walter and Howie, 2011). After all, while some discuss "When China rules" (Jacques, 2009), others are concerned about the spectre of the decreased adequacy of the Chinese party-state to deal with economic institution-building (Guo, 2010).

Market Creation as a Political Process

Markets are institutions setting incentives for actors to pursue their interests (Williamson, 1998; North, 1990; Furubotn and Richter, 1993). They are the product of actions, are embedded in specific socio-cultural contexts, and need consistent supervision, preservation, attention and innovation (Lütz, 2002; Vogel, 1996; Laurence, 2001). They are, therefore, dynamic not only in relation to economic activity but also regarding changes to their institutional settings. Understanding this, market participants follow a dual logic: maximising their interests within the existing framework and pursuing various strategies – most prominently exit and voice (Hirschman, 1970) – to influence changes in the institutional settings. Changes to the framework of markets usually occur incrementally and consistently but sometimes in a more radical ("big bang") fashion. Often they are the result of profound alterations in the external environment (crisis) or a change in political leadership accompanied by or expressing a paradigm shift in market-oriented thinking (Gottwald, 2010). In this regard, crises are ruptures in the developmental path that might weaken path dependencies. In most cases, however, they do not completely terminate the impact of customs, traditions and other unofficial institutions. The recognition that markets and market creation need to be considered as part of a broader socio-political context is usually referred to as the study of the politics of regulation. Such study is closely linked with the interrelated perspectives of the regulatory state and varieties of capitalism (Levi-Faur, 2012a; 2012b), both of which have had a growing influence on the political conceptualisation of, as well as academic research on, China's socialist market economy (Hsueh, 2011; Witt, 2010).

The Chinese way of creating a market in financial services has been recognised as being very significant in the context of the global financial crisis of 2008. The project of globalisation has often been linked with the so-called "Washington Consensus" of market opening and national liberalisation. International bodies are working on the presumption of universally-shared acceptance of certain principles and rules that allow for fair competition for all enterprises, globally and locally. Leaving the issue of fairness and universality aside for a moment, the implementation of global best practice as a near-uniform set of norms, standards and rules has profoundly changed the framework for the operation of financial services. Since the breakdown of Lehman Brothers, however, the pressure to formulate a coherent global crisis response and a new set of rules for global capital has intensified. China has taken a central role in the Group of Twenty (G-20) Finance Ministers and Central Bank Governors, which was established in 1999. It is intent on contributing to the reform of the global architecture for finance (Zhou, 2010) even if its success and its impact on national reform policies are the subject of intense debate among scholars and practitioners (Acharya, 2011; Cooper, 2010; Chin, 2010).

Market Creation within China's Socialism with Chinese Characteristics

Since the late 1970s, the PRC sought to gradually integrate core market mechanisms into its socialist society (Lardy, 2001; Naughton, 2009). According to its Constitution, the "state has put into practice a socialist market economy" (Constitution of the PRC, 2004–08). While most areas of economic activity were allowed to grow out of centralised mandatory planning, the CCP kept a strict hold on the political system and continues to control key sectors of the economy through a mixture of the strategic placement of personnel from the party hierarchy and by selectively controlling access to resources. Since they are also free of constraints that might be presented by the operation of an independent judiciary, local, provincial and central cadres have ample opportunities to push aside private competitors (*guo jin min tui*).

In recent years, Chen Yun's famous "bird cage" description of the Chinese economy has not lost its value. The "cage" – China's socialist framework – might have turned wealthy and huge, but it still remains a serious barrier to freedom for the "bird" (i.e. markets). China's reform policies have been described as the evolution of a distinctively Chinese form of capitalism (McNally, 2007; Breslin, 2007; disputed by Pearson, 2011, p. 41) involving the rise to power of cadre capitalists (Dickson, 2008; Tsai, 2007) who have been adapting to a changing international environment and implementing Western techniques in the "business of governing business" (Pearson, 2007). China's socialist market economy has been said to exhibit an "institutional amphibiousness" (Ding, 1994): a market-oriented system based on strong involvement of a one-party state that controls the judiciary, the media and most of the large enterprises through a system of partial ownership of firms, control of top management positions and privileged access to finance. Overall, the two key pillars of the socialist market economy are the public ownership of enterprises in the economic realm and the leading role of the CCP in politics. This process of institutional change exhibits various patterns, linking domestic imperatives with international drivers of change (Breslin, 2007). The most notable of these international drivers was China's admission to the WTO, which forced the Chinese leadership to balance the interests of important groups and factions inside the party-state with the need to adopt global norms and standards (Hsueh, 2011).

There should be no doubt about the tremendous degree of change within the Chinese one-party state, but let us be under no illusions that the progress has been uniform across all aspects of governance. Still absent are any signs of progress towards a democratic multi-party system representing differing interests within the society and the implementation of a rule of law guaranteeing individual freedoms and private property rights. Changes take place only within the limits set by the CCP-dominated and CCP-controlled Leviathan (Yang, 2005). The issue of whether China's socialist market economy meets Western market standards is a highly political one. The EU flatly refuses to grant market-economy status to this form of "cadre capitalism" (Heilmann, 1996) on the grounds that China is not fulfilling the relevant criteria (Remond, 2007). In international comparison, entrepreneurial freedom in China is average at best (World Bank, 2010).

The CCP has managed to preserve and even strengthen its grip on power by successfully co-opting new elites (Dickson, 2008; Tsai, 2007). This includes the rebuilding of party committees in enterprises and social organisations (Shambaugh, 2007). The CCP provides access to entrepreneurial opportunities and economic rents. The party controls the elites in politics, administration, law, major enterprises and important societal organisations. While pursuing ambitious reforms of the legal system and proclaiming the objective of rule of law in China, there are only limited attempts to bring the CCP under the control of the judiciary. Thus, the Chinese legal system aims at rule by law rather than rule of law (Peerenboom, 2002; Li, 2013).

The Policies: Creating Capital Markets within China's Socialist Market Economy

The 1997/98 financial crisis in East Asia is usually considered a watershed in China's attempts to reform its financial system (Naughton, 2007). China's leaders had left financial services outside their reform policies for a relatively long time. The first official stock exchanges were opened in 1990/91 in Shenzhen and Shanghai as a direct response to increased speculation through China's vibrant underground banking system. Following the usual reform pattern of the Deng Xiaoping era, access to both stock exchanges remained strictly limited. Provincial governments had a key role in the selection of those enterprises that were allowed to pursue listings. These provided ample opportunities for individual and local enrichment and strengthened the asymmetry between investors and enterprises in China's stock markets (Heilmann and Gottwald, 2002). Famously, China's stock markets were compared to casinos with the tongue-in-cheek qualification that gambling houses generally operate according to a set of rules.

China's state-owned banks were slowly transformed into specialist commercial banks. At first they were refinanced by the government and then, in 2004/05, opened to foreign investment (Allen et al., 2012; Gottwald and Schlichting, 2005; Schlichting, 2008). Substantial areas of its banking and insurance market, however, are still closed for foreign investment (OECD, 2005; Huang Hui, 2010). The originally single Bank of China has meanwhile been split and one part has been transformed into a central bank – the People's Bank of China (PBC). Using the means of the Leninist party-apparatus, a Central Work Group was set up and national conferences were held to promote the cause of and develop a strategy for a revision of China's regulatory and supervisory structure. The objective was clear – to reform the state-owned banks that were caught in a mutual destructive relationship with large and predominantly loss-making state-owned enterprises without giving too much room for foreign and domestic speculation (Okazaki, 2007).

These policies followed two conflicting imperatives: to establish viable, open and stable markets and, at the same time, to solve the financial problems of China's state-owned enterprises (Heilmann, 2002). Heavy support for the biggest banks, all owned and controlled by the central government, led to the establishment of an unbalanced financial system consisting of four commercial banks under the control of the central government – the Bank of China (BOC), the China Construction Bank (CCB), the Agricultural Bank of China (ABC) and the Industrial and Commercial Bank of China (ICBC). These banks were set up between 1979 and 1984, thus ending the era of a single bank administering credit and taking the functions of a central bank between 1949 and 1979. In 1994, three specialist policy banks were spun off these banks to separate political and business oriented operations: China Development Bank, Agricultural Development Bank of China and China Export-Import Bank (Huang Hui, 2010). Together with several banks on the provincial and local levels that are generally established as joint stock companies of private and public funds, they constitute the "Big 4" of China's financial system (Martin, 2012). The introduction of two stock exchanges in Shenzhen and Shanghai in 1990/91 and the introduction of various other markets for bonds etc. were closely linked with efforts to put the state-owned enterprises on a more stable footing. Trading the shares of meticulously selected enterprises initially nominated by provincial governments on the stock exchanges provided an alternative venue for financing and took at least some of the burden off the commercial banks (Heilmann, 2002). The introduction of large insurance companies and several securities-related businesses complemented the emergence of a "typical" market-style financial sector in China. Hopes by the government that these steps would lead to a diffusion of China's large underground banking system seem to have been over-optimistic. Shadow banking and illegal provision of credit continue to play a vital role particularly for the private sector, which finds itself at a strategic disadvantage against companies run by the state. In some areas, such as Wenzhou, underground banking gained a significance that led to various efforts to bring the illegal operations into the official banking sector.

When pursuing these reforms, the PRC benefited from several distinct advantages: a high savings rate; the proximity to Hong Kong with its experienced and advanced banking sector and globally significant stock exchange; high foreign investment into the Chinese economy; the ability of the inner-party apparatus to secure control of personnel and access to significant resources; control of the media and the courts; and the size and significance of state-owned enterprises. Three sets of policies stood out. The government changed the regulatory framework emulating Western agencification; strengthened and stabilised the balance sheets of its main commercial banks through a series of direct transfers from the state coffers; and turned central administrative units into special vehicles for global portfolio investment, adding another area for direct competition between China's financial service enterprises and their governmental principals to the financial system.

The characteristics of China's political order with the central role of the CCP leadership left a distinctive mark on the reform process. In the wake of the reforms, however, it emerged that these policies created significant new challenges for the central government and new leeway for local authorities. They encouraged policy-driven credit expansion and the increased global role of China's finance. This tested the capacity of the central government to control the developments (Ong, 2012).

The Outcomes: Regulatory Agencies, the Central Bank and Self-Regulation in the Context of the Party-State

In the period between 1948 and 1978, the Chinese leadership abolished the remnants of a private financial sector as part of its attempts to follow first the Soviet model of a centrally administered economy and then the Maoist ideal of socioeconomic development through mass mobilisation. All functions that in market economies are divided between central banks, regulatory authorities and commercial entities were concentrated within the PBC. With the beginning of the policies of reform and opening up, the PBC was formally given a certain degree of independence. Following a global trend, regulatory reforms in China brought three major changes:

- the complete overhaul of the central bank system, which freed the regional branches from the interference of provincial governments (Yang, 2005);
- the foundation and dissolution of the Central Finance Work Commission; and
- the introduction of the China Securities Regulatory Commission (CSRC), the China Banking Regulatory Commission (CBRC) and the China Insurance Regulatory Commission (CIRC).

As detailed accounts of the introduction and working of these commissions have been provided elsewhere (Green, 2003; Naughton, 2009), the following analysis will focus on the specific content and organisation of governance.

The CSRC, CBRC and CIRC are "institutions under the State Council", the Chinese government, as is the PBC. They are officially part of the central government. Even the PBC must implement the policies of the State Council, seek and follow its advice in important matters, and have its leaders appointed by the State Council and the National People's Congress. As a result, nearly all of their senior and mid-level staff are ranked party members.

The PBC has lost staff and some competencies to the new agencies but still remains arguably the most powerful organisation in the regulation of financial services. Its mission statement still gives it the responsibility for the general regulation of financial services, including the inter-bank markets and the preservation of financial stability. In addition to these regulatory agencies, China created the State-owned Assets Administration and Supervision Commission (SASAC) in 2002/04 (Naughton, 2007),[2] widened the role of the State Administration of Foreign Exchange (SAFE) and set up its first official sovereign wealth fund, the China Investment Corporation (CIC).

The regulatory authorities are trusted with the objective of prudential regulation as well as code of conduct supervision. In established market economies, regulatory agencies are complemented by independent self-regulatory bodies. The Chinese case differs significantly. The rising number of business organisations, sectoral bodies etc. notwithstanding, the regulatory bodies control the governing bodies of these organisations and, thereby, blur the lines between regulatory agencies and self-regulatory bodies (Huang Hui, 2010). Other important elements that are considered a prerequisite to the US-European model of regulation – an independent judiciary, a free press and unfettered representation of consumer interests – are also absent (Gottwald and Collins, 2012). In its formal sectoral organisation, the Chinese regulatory regime has been strongly influenced by the US model. It thus incorporates the concept of regulatory competition between various organisations. In addition, it raises the issue of how to coordinate the work of sectoral bodies and their supplements vis-à-vis their political principals and a growing number of integrated products and financial service conglomerates (Huang, 2009).

Regulatory competition is considered a rather useful instrument at least in some cases. It stems partly from the incremental approach the Chinese government took towards economic-system reform. After several rounds of enterprise reforms, the SASAC is still in charge of central-owned enterprises. It has the power to regulate, among other things, overseas investments. But even in its official statements, it hints at the problems of ensuring compliance with its rules by lower-level supervisory bodies (Jiang, 2011).

Due to the occasionally opaque system of governance, rumours are rife of pending changes to the regulatory structure. One consideration that has gained traction during the financial crisis is the establishment of a ministerial-level body overseeing all central government controlled financial services providers following the SASAC model for industry. At an earlier stage, Central Huijin Investment Ltd., the domestic investment arm of China's sovereign wealth fund, had taken on similar functions without unifying control in its hands; instead becoming part of the broader turf war between the various organisations within central-level government. Coordination between the various bodies is provided at the highest level by the State Council, in National Finance Work Conferences and through the Joint Conference on Financial Supervision, but it is often considered to be insufficient. Thus, every now and then the establishment of a new superior body that would either integrate or supersede the other regulatory bodies finds its way into public discourse (Lim and Koh, 2011; He, 2004). A new ministerial-level super-regulator would at least allow the party rank held by its president to be raised, thus helping to overcome the common problem that most regulatory heads face: their opposite numbers in business outrank them in the party hierarchy. To be effective, a regulator needs to be led by a Vice-Prime Minister to establish the necessary authority of the regulator, but even an upgrade of this scope would not necessarily solve the issue of informal status. An increasing number of financial conglomerates, banks and private equity firms are run by "princelings": family members of very prominent CCP cadres. These well-connected and well-networked "princelings" are able to mobilise substantial political clout beyond their official party rank. Thus, even the most powerful weapon in the arsenal of the party-state, the reliance on party hierarchy, has begun to lose its effectiveness: central cadre control by the party-organs is increasingly compromised by the political power of revolutionary families (Cheng, 2012).

The Many Faces of the CCP in China's Financial Markets

The specific path of market creation by Leninist means has created a unique situation. The CCP has allowed a quasi-private market in financial services to emerge while preserving for itself considerable influence in all areas of the market through the cadre management of the party, control of substantial funds and integration of the regulatory authorities into the party-state apparatus. It appoints and assesses the top managers of the biggest banks, exchanges, intermediaries, regulators, the media and the judiciary. It also owns substantial shares in all major financial service companies, directs credit and decides about venues for recapitalisation. In addition, it sets funding requirements and options and controls foreign access into the market as well as outward investments. The party sets and enforces the scope for investigative journalism and reporting. The CCP wears many hats and has many faces in the context of financial services. It would be wrong, however, to assume total control as different interests within the party-state and difficulties in enforcing central policies on the ground act as an important counterweight against central party control.

The degree to which the regulatory agencies are fully embedded into the party-state has been amply demonstrated. The party-state selects the leading managers, decides staffing levels and sets up party groups (Heilmann, 2005; Pearson, 2007). Nevertheless, their establishment led to closer links with the global regulatory communities and changes in the content of regulation (Schlichting, 2008). Different systems within the State Council and conflicting interests between key players, particularly the Ministry of Finance and the PBC, add another degree of opacity to the regulation of China's finance industry. In high-profile cases, such as the activities of SAFE and the CIC or the responsibility for the oversight of the remaining central government owned companies, conflicts of interest have been documented (Walter and Howie, 2011, pp. 127–38; Heep, 2014, pp. 46–49). The dual functions of the PBC as a vehicle of government policies – including the financing of the largest commercial banks and the financing of China's enormous foreign exchange reserves – mean it is much more heavily involved in the actual market place than would be good for a guardian of system stability. Its exposure to debt has reached levels that have caused some observers to speculate about a hidden insolvency of the PBC (Chang, 2011).

In addition to the three regulatory agencies, the powerful National Development and Reform Commission (NDRC), the Ministry of Finance, SASAC, the PBC and Central Huijin Investment Ltd. are all involved in policy-making and implementation in the area of financial services. The handling of everyday issues, such as dealing with non-performing loans within China's banking system, has been likened to a family business moving assets around the various organisations without significantly reducing, let alone resolving, the problem (Walter and Howie, 2011). The CCP controls human resources management for top positions in all regulatory bodies and defines policy goals. Besides, the CCP steers the party committees within the enterprises, whose re-establishment seems to have accelerated under the government of Wen Jiabao. Top enterprise leaders have party-ranks equalling ministerial levels.

Formally, the highest authority for the supervision of financial services in China, especially the control of the supervisors, rests with the State Council. It defines the general political aims for the development and regulation of financial services for the administrative market supervisors and self-regulatory bodies. Of course, the State Council has to adhere to the fundamental guidelines of overall economic and social policies – financial market regulation is perceived as a means to promote economic growth and social development rather than to be an end in itself. In both the formulation of economic policies and the regulation financial services, supra-ministerial commissions rather than single ministers have played a crucial role.

The National People's Congress (NPC), while the ultimate organ for policy-making according to the Constitution of the PRC, is comparatively weak in real terms. It has gained significance as a forum for discourse and lobbying and, in some instances, has used its role as a lawmaker to influence the distribution of gains and losses by setting "technical" standards. "[T]he NPC can be placed on a continuum of legislatures even if at the less powerful end" (Collins and Cottey, 2012, p. 73). In relation to financial services, the legislature is clearly much less central as a forum for policy discussions than the Politburo and its National Finance Work Conference, a high-profile event held every five years to outline central policies for the sector. Main policies are coordinated by the Leading Small Group on Finance and Economics, which brings together the foremost cadres from the Central Committee, the State Council, the ministries and other significant agencies (Miller, 2008). It contrasts sharply with the unified appearance of a one-party state. While the party machinery can be extremely efficient in dealing with specific challenges – such as the 2008 crisis – it has proven much less coherent when dealing with the incremental development of the regulatory framework. For external observers, it has been a regular phenomenon that issues that have long been under consideration are suddenly abandoned in favour of unexpected new regulations. Fair participation and transparency in the workings of the regulatory bodies are one core principle of the modern regulatory state. Yet they are hardly evolving in the PRC.

The close integration of the banking sector into the party-state became obvious during the current financial crisis: first, the Chinese leadership stimulated and then reined in the provision of credit by Chinese banks through informal telephone calls. Second, a conference of the main regulatory bodies led to a new policy linking the financial services industry in China to the overall strategy of promoting Chinese enterprises abroad, the so-called "Go Global" strategy. In sum, the close relationship between the party and the financial industry is pervasive and persistent (Anderlini, 2009; He, 2010).

The concentration of control in the hands of the party-state adds more structural flaws. All regulatory bodies are subject to intensive lobbying, but in the case of China privileged links to top party officials provide alternative venues for both influencing market activities and pursuing political objectives. The state controls the credit volume and the interest banks are allowed to pay and to accept. Cautious steps to liberalise the interest rate regime pose a fundamental challenge to the Big 4 whose business model is not yet tuned to the demands of market competition. Their profitability rests heavily on low fixed interest rates. The declared objective of the State Council to overcome the monopoly by inducing more competition stretches the resources of the Big 4 with regard to risk management and assessment of business activity (Barboza, 2012). In a market environment where the turn-over of personnel is already extremely high, the introduction of market-based risk assessment poses an insurmountable challenge. These steps are necessary, however, to fulfil the political aim of establishing the Renminbi Yuan as a global – i.e. freely convertible – currency.

The state controls admission to the stock markets and the most important investors. In spite of constitutional safeguards for private property, private investors act de facto under the uncertainty of unstable and unreliable property rights. While media reporting has improved and several series of investigative articles have led to the detection of scandals and fraud, there is only limited independent control of market activities through intermediaries and news magazines which are considered crucial elements of a working market environment. The lack of independent media reporting might help to explain why the true costs of recapitalising banks in the 1990s went more or less unnoticed by larger parts of the Chinese population in spite of the fact that it constituted a "very large transfer of wealth from households to banks and borrowers" (Pettis, 2011). When dealing with the fallout from the 2008 financial crisis, the party hierarchy ensured that phone calls to important managers expressed support for the policies of the day such as the extension of credit, even at the risk of producing significant amounts of non-performing loans, or the calling back of credit (including that of international customers).

Due to different strands of political control of the individual organisations, conflicting interests at the top level can slow down and counteract the party levers. Factional politics play an important role in translating domestic and external developments into institutional change (Shih, 2007). Particularly in the case of dealing with local investment vehicles, the central government was apparently unaware of the high volume of debts resulting from speculation in property and has found it difficult to rein in credit growth, either by macroeconomic regulation or by party mechanisms. Besides, while political lines of hierarchy are clear on paper, it is not specified whether the central government has ultimately to guarantee local government debt or which mechanisms should be employed to resolve issues (Orlik, 2011). Yet even if these issues were clarified, competing interests within the state create an environment of conflicting policy options that allow local policy entrepreneurs to seek their advantage. The interest of reining in local investments to flatten a pending property bubble after 2009 stood in sharp contrast to the need of local governments to create income through the reallocation of land (Li, 2013). With the selection of a new party leadership in 2012, the leeway for local cadres was substantial. Issues of financial market creation were thus linked to fiscal and, through the convertibility of the Renminbi, even to global economic policy issues. This underlines the costs resulting from China's incremental approach to creating a market in financial services: political responsibility and financial accountability are hard to establish.

The External Dimension: Market Creation and Integration into Global Markets

Since its entry into the WTO, China has increasingly adopted global norms and standards, despite deliberately obfuscating the domestic implementation of important elements of the WTO agreement. In financial services, it has come a long way towards accepting global standards and principles, with foreign investments into Chinese lenders playing an important role in this process (Schlichting, 2008; Pistor, 2009). Nevertheless, its incremental policies of market creation required a careful case-by-case approach towards global governance. The piecemeal opening up of the Chinese market to foreign banks and the divestment of large global players from China highlights the difficult balance between using foreign funds, expertise and know-how for domestic development and preserving control of key elements of the sector.

Following the pattern of intensive study and meticulous consideration before committing to multilateral initiatives, the Chinese leadership needed a substantial amount of time to define its position on global crisis management. During late 2008 and the beginning of 2009, China used all its channels of bilateral and multilateral cooperation to define its policies. At the Washington Summit in November 2008, President Hu Jintao stressed the need for close cooperation and a fundamental review of global rules but with due respect to individual circumstances. At the same time, he warned against premature moves (FMPRC, 2008) and tried to buy time for the complicated policy-making process in Beijing. China's leaders were careful not to echo voices from China's domestic discussions calling for Chinese redefinition of the global order (Shao, 2008; Dyer, 2009).

For the party-state, an increased role in the revision of global governance conflicts with several principles and interests. First, the PRC takes economic security very seriously and considers economic sovereignty an absolute precondition for successful modernisation. Hence, the G-20 proposal to install a global banking regulator with authority over Chinese banks is deemed unacceptable. Second, it acknowledges the intrinsic link between global and domestic reforms; the international level, therefore, should support the improvement of the market framework with Chinese characteristics but not destabilise the complex web of party involvement (Niquet, 2009). One of the main – and less risky – objectives of China's policies in the context of the G-20 is to ensure it sits at the table when all new rules and policies are drafted. Consequently, it has pushed for a stronger representation in the Bretton Woods organisations and other global financial bodies. High-ranking officials had repeatedly stressed the crucial importance of reforming the IMF in the context of global crisis management (Drezner, 2009, pp. 32–33; Gottwald, 2011). At the same time, China was among the first countries to adopt – at least nominally – severe Basel III standards. It committed to the review process of the G-20 and the Financial Stability Board regarding its governance structure and implementation of policies. This could increase foreign influence on the continuation of market development in China. The substance of these policies notwithstanding, they signal an increased awareness of the greater role Chinese banks and government representatives are set to play in the aftermath of the 2008 GFC (Rana, 2013).

The extent to which China's unique approach to market creation can be accommodated within a new global framework has come to the fore as an issue in the reform of the Financial Stability Forum (FSF), which had been set up to coordinate selected policies in global finance. In April 2009, the FSF was transformed into the Financial

Stability Board (FSB), a potentially powerful tool for transnational supervision of national finance systems. The FSF had had very little success in promoting global rules and codes of conduct in financial services prior to the global financial crisis of 2008, but subsequently took a central role in identifying and addressing key contributing factors (Carrasco, 2010). Emerging markets were not represented: homogeneity was deemed more efficient than inclusion by major nations.

The PRC supported the establishment of the FSB and joined it despite being well aware that this step increased the pressure to adopt international standards. Accordingly, domestic voices called for the establishment of a Chinese financial stability board to support the State Council in the supervision of the financial system and to improve coordination among the existing supervisory authorities. These proposals are opposed by the PBC, which wants to preserve its authority in the area of macro-prudential supervision (Zhou, 2010). In the view of some observers, the mandate for the FSB "present[s] significant threats to national sovereignty, as it gives the international community the authority to review and regulate the financial and operational structures of private enterprises, potentially bypassing the jurisdiction of national regulatory systems" (Kelly, 2009). The PRC has already in general accepted the principle of peer reviews of regulation and regulatory reforms with the explicit aim of introducing a race to the top regarding the quality of regulation (G-20, 2010). In this regard, the FSB follows similar procedures within the G-20, but all measures decided by the G-20 need unanimity, thereby leaving room for a veto. Calls for the introduction of new banking levies and a global transaction tax were vetoed, to the disappointment of EU leaders. The PRC leadership seems to trust the weak institutional set-up of the FSB (Kawai and Pomerleano, 2009), thinking that this should leave enough room for a preservation of the Chinese characteristics in the regulation of financial services.

Conclusion

The piecemeal approach of the Chinese party-state to the creation of a market in financial services followed the over-arching interests of the CCP in preserving and focusing their influence within a market-oriented framework for economic activity. This approach dovetails nicely with the observation that the PRC has not just established another version of the regulatory state but that it has used the main characteristics of this internationally accepted paradigm to further improve its socialist market economy. This step-by-step introduction of reforms, experiments with various models, learning and adaptation can all be recognised in China's financial system. The central role of party organisation and control of financial resources are balanced by an increasing diversity of interests within the party-state. The image of an all-pervasive party-state is thus countered by bureaucratic turf wars and piecemeal and uncertain implementation of policies.

Unless a major crisis unites the leadership and allows for a combination of the better of two worlds – a state of the art regulatory apparatus and the powerful instruments of top-down Leninist party hierarchy – reform will be slow. The campaign-style provision of extra credit in the context of the macroeconomic stimulus package proved to be much easier than the retrenchment that was supposed to follow. Central authorities seem to be particularly successful in steering their provincial and local counterparts into action when the latter reap direct benefits. The issue of who will have to foot the bill for excessive spending and lending, however, is far from clear and will provide another important case study of the interplay of market and party-state forces in China's finance system.

Three decades of market creation in the area of financial services have left China with some of the largest banks in the world. Their shares are traded internationally yet still dominated by state guidance and party control. While the strong state involvement and strict limits to business activities have protected China's financial sector against the worst fall-out from the current global crisis, they have preserved substantial flaws.

Due to the long experience of dealing with commercial banks that are close to local and provincial cadres, the century-old underground banking system continues to flourish. Even in localities famous for their bottom-up development of export-oriented industries, such as Wenzhou, local business owners still engage with alternative sources of credit that are completely outside the official regulatory structure. Yet even where the party-state officially occupies the commanding heights of the society, it finds it increasingly difficult to rein in creative financing vehicles set up by local authorities to benefit from China's rampant property speculation.

Having been cut off from alternative funding by the central government, China's lower-level authorities have invested heavily in property and property-related areas during the macroeconomic stimulus package. The exact amount of credit amassed by different sorts of special vehicles stunned the central authorities and was first reported in the Chinese media with reference to the US scholar Victor Shih. In the typical learning-by-doing bureaucratic policy process, the central government took several steps to improve oversight of these funding vehicles while at the same time ensuring the domestic as well as the foreign audience of the limited risk these developments are supposed to hold for the Chinese economy as a whole. This adds to an increasing awareness of the peculiar strategy and style in addressing issues within China's financial sector that is radically criticised for its focus on internal dealings and party-state control.

China's way of creating markets in financial services hardly offers a blueprint for other economies. Some states with a similar party-state structure might feel encouraged by the initial success of China's reform policies, yet they lack the size, attractiveness and, in particular, a gate such as Hong Kong to emulate the Chinese reforms. Preserving and improving state involvement and state control within the formal framework of a regulatory state model, however, has become the fashion in post-2008 crisis management. Most European countries and the US have taken significant steps in re-introducing and strengthening public authority within the private realm of financial services. China has been called upon to take a more active role and provide leadership in these global efforts due to its economic size, the capacity of its biggest banks and investment vehicles and its limited crisis exposure. But taking into account the specific nature of the Chinese gradual policies to set up markets to enforce – and by no means replace – party-state guidance and control of the financial sector, the PRC had little choice but to dampen down over-optimistic expectations regarding its future role in global governance. While the strong role of the party-state is a key characteristic of the overall economic development path of the PRC, we should be careful not to prematurely link these developments with the broad China Model debate. The financial services sector exhibits very specific characteristics and defies simple generalisations.

The integration into the global economy has increased the pressure on the PRC to create a market framework that allows for global standards, norms and business practices to take (partial) root in its socialist market economy. While initially China had to adapt to rules decided upon in forums and organisations where the PRC yielded little influence, the Chinese leadership has made it clear that it is sitting right at the head of the table in the current effort to find a new architecture for financial services. Again, the Chinese leadership has to accept that joining the global community limits its domestic policy choices. Hence the old dichotomy between attempts to preserve the original Chinese structure or essence (*ti*) while adopting external practices and technology (*yong*) is currently at play. Globally, the PRC hesitantly participates in the new regulatory framework for financial markets. At home, it tries to balance conflicting interests within its government and between different market participants. This increases the dynamic of seeking individual gain in the area of financial services – the basic concept of a market economy.

Despite the process of adjustment to both global imperatives and unparalleled economic development, the basic shape of the PRC's Leninist *modus operandi* remains intact. Regulatory reforms have been introduced through traditional hierarchical Leninist institutions and, just as in other areas, lower-level cadres have been able to blunt their impact. Nevertheless, one-party rule, state domination of the economy and an adroit use of ideological rhetoric are key features of China's market creation by Leninist means. Non-state actors may aspire to important secondary roles but the CCP diva commands the stage.

Notes

1. Reminiscent of the famous *ti-yong* debate of late nineteenth-century China.
2. The law on SASAC was passed in 2002 and first measures were promulgated informally in the name of SASAC, which officially started work in 2004. See www.sasac.gov.cn.

References

Acharya, Amitav (2011) Can Asia lead? Power ambitions and global governance in the twenty-first century. *International Affairs* 87(4), pp. 851–69.

Allen, Franklin, Jun "QJ" Qian, Chenying Zhang and Mengxin Zhao (2012) *China's financial system: Opportunities and challenges. NBER Working Paper Series*, Working Paper 17828. Available at http://www.nber.org/papers/w17828, accessed 20 December 2012.

Anderlini, James (2009) Rule of the iron rooster. Financial Times Online, 24 August. Available at http://www.ft.com/cms/s/0/ae083ef2-90de-11de-bc99-00144feabdc0.html?SID=google, accessed 15 February 2010.

Barboza, David (2012) Wen calls China's banks too powerful. New York Times Online, 3 April. Available at http://www.nytimes.com/2012/04/04/business/global/chinas-big-banks-too-powerful-premier-says.html?adxnnl=1&adxnnlx=1361455309-1wnUwVfaQeDnE1FhfJY+aw, accessed 12 September 2012.

Breslin, Shaun (2007) *China and the global political economy* (Basingstoke: Palgrave Macmillan).

Carrasco, Enrique R. (2010) The global financial crisis and the financial stability forum: The awakening and transformation of an international body. *Transnational Law & Contemporary Problems* 19, pp. 203–20.

Chang, Gordon C. (2011) Is the People's Bank of China insolvent? Forbes Online, 17 April. Available at http://www.forbes.com/sites/gordonchang/2011/04/17/is-the-peoples-bank-of-china-insolvent/2/, accessed 9 October 2012.

Cheng, Li (2012) The battle for China's top nine leadership posts. *The Washington Quarterly* 35(1), pp. 131–45.

Chin, Gregory (2010) The emerging countries and China in the G-20: Reshaping global economic governance. *Studia Diplomatica* 63(2), pp. 105–23.
Collins, Neil and Andrew Cottey (2012) *Understanding Chinese politics* (Manchester: Manchester University Press).
Constitution of the People's Republic of China. Full text after amendment on 14 March 2004. Available at http://www.npc.gov.cn/englishnpc/Constitution/node_2825.htm, accessed 5 September 2014.
Cooper, Andrew F. (2010) The G-20 as an improvised crisis committee and/or a contested "steering committee". *International Affairs* 86(3), pp. 741–57.
Dickson, Bruce (2008) *Wealth into power: The Communist Party's embrace of China's private sector* (Cambridge: Cambridge University Press).
Ding, Xueliang (1994) Institutional amphibiousness and the transition from Communism: The case of China. *British Journal of Political Science* 24(3), pp. 293–318.
Drezner, David W. (2009) Bad debts. Assessing China's influence on greater power politics. *International Security* 34(2), pp. 7–45.
Dyer, Geoff (2009) Beijing pushed for economic disclosure. *Financial Times*, 2 March. Available at http://www.ft.com/intl/cms/s/0/1eff6064-0759-11de-9294-000077b07658.html#axzz2Tw01dF3l, accessed 12 December 2012.
Foreign Ministry of the PR China (FMPRC) (2008) Hu Jintao addresses the G-20 summit on financial markets and the world economy. Washington, 16 November. Available at http://www.fmprc.gov.cn/eng/wjdt/zyjh/t522600.htm, accessed 17 October 2012.
Furubotn, Eirik and Rudolph Richter (1993) *Neue Institutionenökonomik* (Tübingen: Mohr Siebeck).
G-20 (2010) *Progress report on the economic and financial actions of the previous G-20 summits*, 20 July, prepared by Korea, Chair of the G-20. Available at http://www.g20.org/Documents2010/07/July_2010_G20_Progress_Grid.pdf, accessed 10 December 2010.
Gottwald, Jörn-Carsten (2010) Europe and China: Convergence, politicization, and assertiveness. *East Asia* 27 (1), pp. 79–97.
Gottwald, Jörn-Carsten (2011) Cadre capitalism goes global: Financial market reforms and the new role of the People's Republic of China in world markets, in Louis Brennan (ed.), *The emergence of southern multinationals and their impact on Europe*, pp. 283–300 (Basingstoke: Palgrave Macmillan).
Gottwald, Jörn-Carsten and Neil Collins (2012) The Chinese model of regulatory state, in David Levi-Faur (ed.), *Handbook on the politics of regulation*, pp. 142–55 (Cheltenham: Edward Elgar).
Gottwald, Jörn-Carsten and Svenja Schlichting (2008) Creating a regulatory regime within Leninist authoritarianism: Financial market reforms in the PRC. Paper presented at the Association of Asian Studies Annual Conference, Atlanta, April.
Green, Stephen (2003) *China's stockmarket: A guide to its progress, players and prospects* (London: Economist Intelligence Unit).
Guo, Rongxing (2010) *An introduction to the Chinese economy. The driving forces behind modern day China* (Singapore: Wiley).
He, Ming (2004) Huijin: A SASAC for China's financial sector? Chatham House Briefing Note, Royal Institute of International Affairs, Asia Program. Available at http://www.isn.ethz.ch/isn/Digital-Library/Publications/Detail/?ots591=eb06339b-2726-928e-0216-1b3f15392dd8&lng=en&id=22991, accessed 9 October 2012.
He Nanfang (2010) *Zhongguo Renmin Yinhang, Zhongguo Yinjianhui, Zhongguo Zhengjianhui, Zhongguo Baojianhui chutai jinyibu zuohao jinrong fuwu zhich zhongdian tiaozheng zhenxing he yizhi bufen xingye channeg guo sheng de zhi.* Available at http://www.gzxz.gov.cn/Article/Print.asp?ArticleID=28688, accessed 20 February 2010.
Heep, Sandra (2014) China in global finance. Domestic financial repression and international financial power (Cham et al.: Springer).
Heilmann, Sebastian (1996) Auf dem Weg zu einer postkommunistischen Gesellschaft: Kaderkapitalismus der VR China. *Zeitschrift für Politik* 43(4), pp. 375–93.
Heilmann, Sebastian (2002) *The Chinese stock market: Pitfalls of a policy-driven market.* China Analysis No. 15, September. Available at www.chinapolitik.de, accessed 10 October 2011.
Heilmann, Sebastian (2005) Regulatory innovation by Leninist means: Communist Party supervision in China's financial industry. *The China Quarterly* 181, pp. 1–21.
Heilmann, Sebastian (2008) From local experiments to national policy: The origins of China's distinctive policy process. *The China Journal* 59, pp. 1–30.

Heilmann, Sebastian and Jörn-Carsten Gottwald (2002) *Der Chinesische Aktienmarkt* (Hamburg: Institute of Asian Affairs).

Herd, Richard, Samuel Hill and Charles Pigott (2010) China's financial sector reforms. Working Paper No. 747. OECD Economics Department. Available at http://www.oecd-ilibrary.org/economics/china-s-financial-sector-reforms_5kmlh5n23mzs-en, accessed 9 October 2012.

Hirschman, Albert O. (1970) *Exit, voice, and loyalty-responses to decline firms, organisations and states* (Cambridge, MA/London: Harvard University Press).

Hsueh, Roselyn (2011) *China's regulatory state. A new strategy for globalization* (Ithaca and London: Cornell University Press).

Huang, Calista (2009) Transformation of China's financial regulatory system under global financial crisis. LINKS Corporate Finance Bulletin, July. Available at http://www.llinkslaw.com/shangchuan/2009710141858.pdf, accessed 9 October 2012.

Huang Hui (2010) Institutional structure of financial regulation in China: Lessons from the global financial crisis. *Journal of Corporate Law Studies* 10(1), pp. 219–54.

Huang, Yasheng, Tony Saich and Edward Saul Steinfeld, eds. (2005) *Financial sector reform in China* (Cambridge, MA: Harvard University Asia Center).

Jacques, Martin (2009) *When China rules the world* (London: Penguin).

Jiang, Jun (2011) SASAC issues regulation on Chinese state-owned overseas assets. Allen & Overy, Shanghai, 4 June. Available at http://www.allenovery.com/publications/en-gb/Pages/SASAC-issues-regulations-on-overseas-state-owned-assets.aspx, accessed 10 October 2011.

Kawai, Masahiro and Michael Pomerleano (2009) International financial stability architecture of the 21st century. *The Financial Times*, 21 August. Available at http://blogs.ft.com/economistsforum/2009/08/international-financial-stability-architecture-for-the-21st-century/, accessed 10 September 2009.

Kelly, Jim (2009) Financial stability board portends global economic governance. *GlobalGovernanceWatch*, 21 April. Available at http://www.globalgovernancewatch.org/spotlight_on_sovereignty/financial-stability-board-portends-economic-global-governance, accessed 10 December 2010.

Lardy, Nicholas (2001) *Integrating China into the global economy* (Washington, DC: Brookings Institution).

Laurence, Henry (2001) *Money rules: The politics of financial regulation in Great Britain and Japan* (London: Cornell University Press).

Levi-Faur, David and Jacint Jordana (2005) Regulatory capitalism: Political irrigants and convergent-divergence, in David Levi-Faur and Jacint Jordana (eds), *The rise of regulatory capitalism: The global diffusion of a new order*, pp. 191–97 (Thousand Oaks: Sage).

Levi-Faur, David (2012a) Regulation and regulatory governance, in David Levi-Faur (ed.), *Handbook on the politics of regulation*, pp. 3–24 (Cheltenham: Edward Elgar Publishing).

Levi-Faur, David (2012b) The regulatory state and regulatory capitalism: An institutional perspective, in David Levi-Faur (ed.), *Handbook on the politics of regulation*, pp. 662–71 (Cheltenham: Edward Elgar Publishing).

Li, Jieli (2013) In transformation toward socio-legality with Chinese characteristics: A critical view, in Li Xiaobing and Qiang Fang (eds), *Modern Chinese legal reforms: New perspectives*, pp. 111–30 (Lexington, KY: Kentucky University Press).

Li, Jing (2013) What causes China's property boom? *Property Management* 31(1), pp. 4–21.

Lim, Benjamin Kam and Koh Gui Qing (2011) Exclusive: China mulls new regulator for state financial sector. Reuters, 3 August. Available at http://www.reuters.com/article/2011/08/03/us-china-regulator-financial-idUSTRE7720LX20110803, accessed 19 March 2011.

Lütz, Susanne (2002) *Der Staat und die Globalisierung der Finanzmärkte* (Frankfurt: Campus).

Martin, Michael F. (2012) *China's banking system: Issues for Congress*. Congress Research Service, 20 February, Washington, DC. Available at www.fas.org/sgp/crs/row/R42380.pdf, accessed 12 December 2012.

Maswana, Jean-Claude (2008) China's financial development and economic growth: Exploring contradictions. *International Research Journal of Finance and Economics* 19, pp. 89–101.

McNally, Christopher (2007) Reflections on capitalism and China's emergent political economy, in Christopher McNally (ed.), *China's emergent political economy: Capitalism in the dragon's lair*, pp. 17–35 (London and New York: Routledge).

Miller, Alice (2008) The Central Committee's leading small groups. *China Leadership Monitor*, No. 26, Fall. Available at http://media.hoover.org/sites/default/files/documents/CLM26AM.pdf, accessed 9 October 2012.

Naughton, Barry (2009) *The Chinese economy: Transition and growth* (London: MIT Press).

Niquet, Valerie (2009) *Public action China: From decision-making to implementation*. Asie Vision No. 14 (Paris: Institut Français des Relations Internationales). Available at www.ifri.org/downloads/AV14_Niquet_ang.pdf, accessed 12 December 2012.

North, Douglas C. (1990) *Institutions, institutional change and economic performance* (Cambridge, MA: Cambridge University Press).

OECD (2005) Governance of banks: China. *Governance China*, pp. 369–402 (Paris: OECD).

Okazaki, Kumiko (2007) Banking system reform in China. The challenges of moving toward a market-oriented economy. Occasional Paper, RAND National Security Research Division. Available at http://www.rand.org/pubs/occasional_papers/2007/RAND_OP194.pdf, accessed 9 October 2012.

Ong, Lynette (2012) Fiscal federalism and soft budget constraints: The case of China. *International Political Science Review* 33(4), pp. 455–74.

Orlik, Tom (2011) China tallies local debt. Wall Street Journal Online, 28 June. Available at http://online.wsj.com/article/SB10001424052702304447804576411013575221104.html, accessed 6 October 2011.

Pearson, Margaret M. (2005) The business of governing business in China: Institutions and norms of the emerging regulatory state. *World Politics* 57(2), pp. 296–325.

Pearson, Margaret M. (2007) Governing the Chinese economy: Regulatory reform in the service of the state. *Public Administration Review* 67(4), pp. 718–30.

Pearson, Margaret (2011) Variety within and without: The political economy of Chinese regulation, in Scott Kennedy (ed.), Beyond the Middle Kingdom: Comparative perspectives on China's capitalist transformation, pp. 25–43 (Stanford: Stanford University Press).

Peerenboom, Randall (2002) China's Long March toward Rule of Law (Cambridge: Cambridge University Press).

Pettis, Michael (2011) The last Chinese banking crisis actually was painful, and the next will be worse. *Business Insider*, 21 January. Available at http://articles.businessinsider.com/2011-01-21/markets/30061253_1_lending-and-deposit-rates-banking-interest-rates, accessed 9 October 2012.

Pistor, Katharina (2009) Banking reform in the Chinese mirror. Institutions and Governance Program, University of California Berkeley. Available at http://igov.berkeley.edu/content/banking-reform-chinese-mirror, accessed 5 September 2014.

Porter, Robin (2011) *From Mao to market: China reconfigured* (New York: Columbia University Press).

Rana, Pradumna B. (2013) From a centralized to a decentralized global economic architecture: An overview. *ADBI Working Paper 401* (Tokyo: Asian Development Bank Institute).

Remond, Michel (2007) The EU's refusal to grant China "Market Economy Status" (MES). *Asia-Europe Journal* 7(5), pp. 34–35.

Schlichting, Svenja (2008) *Internationalising China's financial markets* (Basingstoke: Palgrave Macmillan).

Schlichting, Svenja (2009) Internationalising China's capital markets: Changing actor constellations and emerging transnational professional communities, in Thomas Heberer and Gunter Schubert (eds), *Regime legitimacy in contemporary China: Institutional change and stability*, pp. 153–73 (London and New York: Routledge).

Shao Feng (2008) Jinrong weiji dui guoji guanxi yinxiang ji zhongguo de yingdui. *Shijie Jingji yu Zhengzhi* 12. Available at http://www.21ccom.net/articles/qqsw/zlwj/article_20100120179.html, accessed 7 October 2012.

Shih, Victor (2007) *Factions and finance in China: Elite conflict and inflation* (Cambridge: Cambridge University Press).

Tsai, Kellee S. (2007) *Capitalism without democracy: The private sector in contemporary China* (Ithaca, NY: Cornell University Press).

Tsai, Wen-Hsuan and Nicola Dean (2013) The CCP's learning system: Thought unification and regime adaption. *The China Journal* 69, pp. 87–107.

Vogel, Steven (1996) *Freer markets, more rules* (London: Cornell University Press).

Walter, Carl E. and Fraser T.J. Howie (2011) *Red capitalism: The fragile financial foundation of China's extraordinary rise* (New York: John Wiley).

Williamson, Oliver E. (1998) *The economic institutions of capitalism* (New York, NY: Free Press).

Witt, Michael A. (2010) China: What variety of capitalism? *INSEAD Working Paper 2010/88EPS* (Paris: INSEAD).

World Bank (2010) Ease of doing business in China. *Doing business: Measuring business regulation*. Available at http://www.doingbusiness.org/data/exploreeconomies/china, accessed 17 October 2012.

Yang, Dali (2005) *Remaking the Chinese Leviathan: Market transition and the politics of governance in China* (Stanford, CA: Stanford University Press).

Yeo, Yukyung and Martin Painter (2011) Diffusion, transmutation, and regulatory regime in socialist market economies: Telecoms reform in China and Vietnam. *The Pacific Review* 24(4), pp. 375–95.

Yu, Yongding (2010) The impact of the global financial crisis on the Chinese economy and China's policy responses. *Third World Network Global Economy Series*, No. 25. Available at http://www.twnside.org.sg/title2/ge/ge25.pdf, accessed 5 September 2014.

Zhou Xiaochuan (2010) *Jinrong zhengce dui jinrong weiji de xiangying*. Available at http://www.pbc.gov.cn/publish/goutongjiaoliu/524/2011/20110104191901596935544/20110104191901596935544_.html, accessed 12 January 2012.

Index

For Product Safety Concerns and Information please contact our
EU representative GPSR@taylorandfrancis.com Taylor & Francis
Verlag GmbH, Kaufingerstraße 24, 80331 München, Germany